Scott Foresman
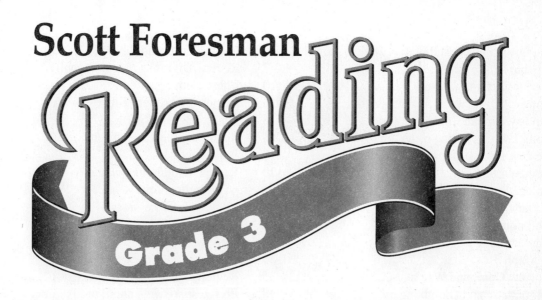

Reading

Grade 3

Phonics Workbook
Blackline Master
and Answer Key

Scott Foresman
Phonics System™

BOWLING GREEN STATE UNIVERSITY
DISCARDED
LIBRARY

Scott Foresman

Editorial Offices: Glenview, Illinois • New York, New York
Sales Offices: Reading, Massachusetts • Duluth, Georgia • Glenview, Illinois
Carrollton, Texas • Menlo Park, California

Editorial Offices: Glenview, Illinois • New York, New York
Sales Offices: Reading, Massachusetts • Duluth, Georgia • Glenview, Illinois
Carrollton, Texas • Menlo Park, California

ISBN 0-673-61432-8

2345678910-CRK-06050403020100

Name_____

CURR
372.4
S42r
/4
gr.3

The letter *a* stands for the short *a* vowel sound in *cat*.
The letter *e* stands for the short *e* vowel sound in *net*.
The letter *i* stands for the short *i* vowel sound in *hit*.

Say each picture name. Write the letter that stands for the vowel sound.

1.  _____

2.  _____

3.  _____

4.  _____

5.  _____

6. _____

7.  _____

8.  _____

9.  _____

10.  _____

Notes for Home: Your child identified the short vowel sounds *a*, *e*, and *i* in picture names.
Home Activity: Together with your child find objects in the room whose names have short vowel sounds. Tell what short vowel sound you hear in each object's name.

1

Name _____

The letter *o* stands for the short *o* vowel sound in *hot*.
The letter *u* stands for the short *u* vowel sound in *luck*.

Underline the words with the same vowel sound as the first word in the row. Then follow the directions.

hot 1. clock   rose   roll   rock

     2. Write two words that rhyme with *hot*.

     _____   _____

run 3. sum   cute   turn   must

     4. Write two words that rhyme with *run*.

     _____   _____

mug 5. count   cut   cup   cube

     6. Write two words that rhyme with *mug*.

     _____   _____

not 7. hold   knob   load   stop

     8. Write two words that rhyme with *not*.

     _____   _____

lock 9. top   pond   bowl   stove

     10. Write two words that rhyme with *lock*.

     _____   _____

Notes for Home: Your child identified words with the short vowel sounds *o* and *u*.
Home Activity: Have your child make up sentences using the words in dark type.

The letters *a, e, i, o,* and *u* stand for the short vowel sounds in words.

| c**a**t | n**e**t | h**i**t | h**o**t | l**u**ck |

Underline two words that have the same short vowel sound as the word at the beginning of the row.

1. trick   lion   quit   shirt   gift

2. spent   next   center   deep   knee

3. stamp   game   salt   stand   after

4. rock   job   home   note   stop

5. just   fur   music   summer   sudden

6. fast   table   band   ask   wait

7. left   each   sleep   empty   set

8. fun   number   excuse   study   fuel

9. cot   coin   enjoy   clock   cannot

10. inch   bike   this   until   time

Notes for Home: Your child identified words with short vowel sounds. **Home Activity:** Have your child choose a favorite book and name words from that book that have short vowel sounds.

3

Name_____

Sometimes the spelling of a base word changes when *-ed* is added.

jump—jump**ed**   no change   chase—cha**sed**   drop the final *e*
clap—clap**ped**   double the final   try—tr**ied**   change *y* to *i*
                  consonant

Write each *-ed* word under the heading that tells what happened to the base word when *-ed* was added.

slipped	relaxed	captured	worried	shared
carried	stopped	played	discovered	studied

No Change   **Dropped the Final *e***

1. _____   4. _____

2. _____   5. _____

3. _____

Doubled the Final Consonant   **Changed *y* to *i***

6. _____   8. _____

7. _____   9. _____

                                     10. _____

Notes for Home: Your child added the *-ed* ending to words. **Home Activity:** Have your child write words that end in *-ed*. Talk about what spelling changes, if any, were needed before the *-ed* ending was added.

4

Name _____

Sometimes the spelling of a base word changes when *-ing* is added.

jump—jump**ing**   no change
smile—smil**ing**   drop the final *e*
hop—hop**ping**   double the final consonant

Add *-ing* to each word. Write the new word on the line.

1. charge _____

2. win _____

3. recite _____

4. discover _____

5. get _____

6. circle _____

7. visit _____

8. strum _____

9. ride _____

10. sing _____

Write the word from above that completes each sentence.

11. On my summer vacation, I will be _____ a ranch.

12. I will be _____ a new pair of cowboy boots for the trip.

13. Each day I will go _____ on a horse.

14. Maybe I will even try _____ a guitar.

15. I will be _____ many new things.

Notes for Home: Your child added the *-ing* ending to words. **Home Activity:** Take turns with your child telling a story about a family trip you would like to take. Use words ending in *-ing*.

5

Some words have double consonants in the middle: *butter, dinner*. The two consonants stand for one sound.

Underline the words with double consonants in the middle.

1. little	**2.** follow	**3.** pepper	**4.** double	**5.** different
6. sorry	**7.** three	**8.** batter	**9.** tomorrow	**10.** kitchen
11. pretty	**12.** forest	**13.** wheel	**14.** happy	**15.** summer

Write the opposite of each word. Use a word from the box.

16. same _____   **17.** salt _____

18. pitcher _____   **19.** lead _____

20. glad _____   **21.** ugly _____

22. big _____   **23.** sad _____

24. today _____   **25.** winter _____

 Notes for Home: Your child identified words with double consonants in the middle.
Home Activity: Have your child choose a word he or she wrote and give another word that has a similar meaning.

Some words have double consonants at the end: *still, gruff*. The two consonants stand for one sound.

Write the two letters that stand for the ending sound in each picture name.

1.  _____

2. 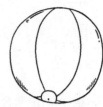 _____

3.  _____

4.  _____

5.  _____

6.  _____

7.  _____

8. _____

9.  _____

10.  _____

 Notes for Home: Your child identified words with double consonants at the end.
Home Activity: Have your child look through a magazine and find other words that have double consonants at the end.

7

Name _____

Review Long *a: a-e*

The *a*-consonant-*e* pattern stands for the long *a* vowel sound.

bake   **same**

Underline each word with the long *a* sound spelled *a*-consonant-*e*. Then use the underlined words to complete the story.

1. made   2. day   3. fame   4. safe

5. way   6. name   7. paid   8. take

9. came   10. trail   11. pale   12. ate

13. Goldilocks is a girl's _____.

14. She gained _____ in a story about three bears.

15. One day she _____ to a house in the woods.

16. She _____ some of the bears' porridge.

17. Goldilocks _____ herself comfortable by sitting in their chairs.

18. Then she tried to _____ a nap.

19. When she saw the bears, she turned _____.

20. She ran from the house until she was _____.

Notes for Home: Your child wrote words with the long *a* vowel sound spelled *a*-consonant-*e*. **Home Activity:** Take turns with your child telling a favorite story. Listen for words with the long *a* sound and name them.

The *i*-consonant-*e* pattern stands for the long *i* vowel sound.

nice   **fine**

Draw a line from each picture to the word for the picture.

1.

dine
dim
dime

2.

fine
five
fire

3.

ride
rice
ripe

4.

pile
pine
pin

5.

prize
prime
price

6.

Mike
mile
mice

7.

bike
bide
bite

8.
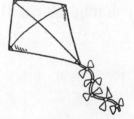
kit
kind
kite

9.

hire
hike
hive

10.
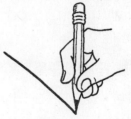
line
life
lime

Notes for Home: Your child identified words with the long *i* vowel sound spelled *i*-consonant-*e*. **Home Activity:** Take turns with your child choosing a long *i* word from the page and making up a silly sentence for the word.

Name_____

The *o-consonant-e* pattern stands for the long *o* vowel sound.

                    w**oke**   h**ope**

Write the word that answers each clue and has the long *o* sound spelled
o-consonant-e.

1. something to wear to keep warm
   robe   coat
   _____

2. a place to live
   house   home
   _____

3. a holder for ice cream
   cone   carton
   _____

4. something a cowhand uses
   rope   road
   _____

5. a beautiful flower
   rose   daffodil
   _____

6. a place to cook
   stove   pot
   _____

7. something you might break if you fall
   bone   toe
   _____

8. where electric wires might be hung
   post   pole
   _____

9. a part of your face
   eyebrows   nose
   _____

10. a way to look at the stars
   window   telescope
   _____

Notes for Home: Your child wrote words with the long *o* vowel sound spelled
o-consonant-e. **Home Activity:** With your child, make up meaning clues for these long *o*
words: *stone, vote, globe, hose.*

The long *e* sound can be spelled *ee, ea, ie,* and *ey*.

teeth	**teach**	**shield**	**donkey**

Follow the directions in each sentence. Choose words from the box.

> movie   reach   cookie   monkey   sweet   feet   beach

1. Write two words that rhyme with *peach*.

_____   _____

2. Circle the way long *e* is spelled in the words you wrote.   ee   ea   ie   ey

3. Change the first letter of *donkey*. Write a word from the box.

_____

4. Circle the way long *e* is spelled in the word you wrote.   ee   ea   ie   ey

5. Write a word for a treat to eat with milk. _____

6. Circle the way long *e* is spelled in the word you wrote.   ee   ea   ie   ey

7. Write two words that rhyme with *meet*.

_____   _____

8. Circle the way long *e* is spelled in the words you wrote.   ee   ea   ie   ey

9. Write a word for what you see on a video.

_____

10. Circle the way long *e* is spelled in the word you wrote.   ee   ea   ie   ey

Notes for Home: Your child wrote words with different spellings for the long *e* sound.
Home Activity: Look through a newspaper together to find words with long *e* spelled *ee, ea, ie,* or *ey*. Circle the words as you find them.

Name _____

The long *e* sound can be spelled *y* or *e*.

busy   me

Underline the words with the long *e* sound spelled *y*. Circle the words with the long *e* sound spelled *e*.

1. excitedly   **2.** she   **3.** zebra

4. buggy   **5.** ugly   **6.** we

7. funny   **8.** maybe   **9.** everybody

Read each sentence. Change the underlined word or words to a word from above. Write the word.

10. Jake had a dog that was <u>not pretty</u>.

_____

11. Everyone thought Jake's dog, Muttsy, was <u>odd</u> looking.

_____

12. When people laughed at her, <u>Muttsy</u> would bark at them.

_____

13. One day Muttsy showed <u>all Jake's friends</u> what a good dog she was.

_____

14. Muttsy kept a baby <u>carriage</u> from rolling into the street.

_____

15. Then all the people cheered <u>frantically</u>.

_____

Notes for Home: Your child wrote words in which the long *e* sound is spelled *y* and *e*.
Home Activity: Together with your child tell a story about a dog. Use some of the long *e* words from the page.

Name _____

The long _e_ sound can be spelled in many different ways.

ee	as in	**f**ee**t**	**ey**	as in	vall**ey**
ea	as in	s**ea**t	**y**	as in	an**y**
ie	as in	**f**ie**ld**	**e**	as in	w**e**

Follow the long _e_ path. In each box, underline two words with the long _e_ sound. Circle the letter or letters that stand for the sound.

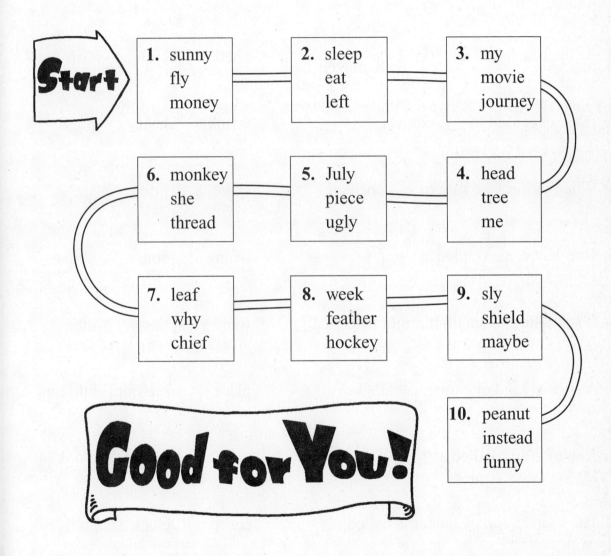

Start

1. sunny
   fly
   money

2. sleep
   eat
   left

3. my
   movie
   journey

4. head
   tree
   me

5. July
   piece
   ugly

6. monkey
   she
   thread

7. leaf
   why
   chief

8. week
   feather
   hockey

9. sly
   shield
   maybe

10. peanut
    instead
    funny

Good for You!

Notes for Home: Your child identified words with different spellings for the long _e_ sound. **Home Activity:** Ask your child think of another long _e_ word for each pattern—_ee, ea, ie, ey, y,_ and _e_.

13

Double consonants may come in the middle or at the end of words. The two letters usually stand for one sound.

    ki**tt**en   mi**rr**or   stu**ff**   se**ll**

Underline the word that completes each sentence and has double consonants.

1. Each morning you must ___.   eat   dress   wash

2. At the beach you might pick up a ___.   shell   crab   fish

3. An iron is used to ___ clothes.   wrinkle   heat   press

4. When writing, be sure to ___ correctly.   write   print   spell

5. One cent is also called a ___.   penny   coin   dollar

6. If something is small, it might be called ___.   wee   tiny   little

7. A special kind of church is called a ___.   place   mission   building

8. A thief is also called a ___.   burglar   robber   crook

9. The sound a turkey makes is called a ___.   cheep   cluck   gobble

10. We had tacos for ___.   breakfast   lunch   dinner

Notes for Home: Your child identified words with double consonants in the middle or at the end. **Home Activity:** Have your child read the underlined words and write another sentence for each one.

Name _____

Words may have double consonants in the middle as in the word *muffin* or at the end as in the word *still*. The two consonants stand for one sound.

Follow each set of directions. Use the words in the box.

scissors	pretty	sheriff	call	full
cliff	pillow	dollar	fuzz	little

Write two words that end like *bell*.

1. _____

2. _____

Write two words that have two *t*'s in the middle like *kitten*.

3. _____

4. _____

Write two words that have two *l*'s like the word *follow*.

5. _____

6. _____

Write two words that end like *stuff*.

7. _____

8. _____

Write another word with two *s*'s in the middle like the word *mission*.

9. _____

Write another word that ends like *jazz*.

10. _____

Notes for Home: Your child identified and wrote words with double consonants in the middle and at the end. **Home Activity:** With your child, look through a favorite book. Take turns pointing to and naming other words with double consonants.

15

The letters *ai* and *ay* stand for the long *a* vowel sound.

wait**   d**ay**

Write each word in the box under the picture whose name has the same pattern for long *a* as the word.

gray	drain	paid	trail	way
stay	braid	rain	play	snail
paint	today	may	train	hay

1. _____

2. _____

3. _____

4. _____

5. _____

6. _____

7. _____

8. _____

9. _____

10. _____

11. _____

12. _____

13. _____

14. _____

15. _____

Notes for Home: Your child wrote words in which the long *a* sound is spelled *ai* or *ay*.
Home Activity: Together use pairs of words from the box to make up rhymes.

The letters *oa, ow,* and *o* stand for the long *o* sound.

b**oa**t   sh**ow**   g**o**

Write the letter or letters that stand for the long *o* sound in each word. Then use the words to complete the ads.

1. coat _____   **2.** bowl _____

3. gold _____   **4.** go _____

5. soap _____   **6.** groan _____

7. mow _____   **8.** auto _____

9. throat _____   **10.** snow _____

11.

ON SALE TODAY! Beautiful _____ Necklaces

12.

Come to TONY'S for a _____ of tasty Spaghetti

13.

DoesYour _____ Need New Brakes? Go to SALLY'S Repair Shop

14.
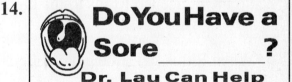
Do You Have a Sore _____? Dr. Lau Can Help

15.
Need Your Grass Cut? I _____ Lawns! Call Me at 555-1814

Notes for Home: Your child wrote words in which the long *o* sound is spelled *oa, ow,* or *o*.
Home Activity: With your child, look at some newspaper ads. Try to find words with long *o* spelled *oa, ow,* or *o*.

The long *a* sound can be spelled *ai* and *ay*. **rain** **hay**

The long *o* sound can be spelled *oa*, *ow*, and *o*. **boat** **show** **gold**

Find the word in each sentence that has the long *a* or long *o* sound. Write the word and circle the letters that stand for the long *a* or long *o* vowel sound.

1. A long time ago there lived a prince. _____

2. He had a pet goat called Rufus. _____

3. Rufus liked to play in the queen's garden. _____

4. He would sneak in and slowly eat all the flowers. _____

5. The prince would groan when he saw what
   Rufus had done. _____

6. One day the prince had a plan. _____

7. He could not wait to try his idea. _____

8. So the prince led Rufus to the big front lawn. _____

9. When Rufus saw all the dandelions, he
   wiggled his tail happily. _____

10. Now Rufus is the best lawn mower
    for the palace. _____

Notes for Home: Your child identified and wrote words with the long *a* and *o* vowel sounds.
Home Activity: With your child, tell another story about the prince and the goat. Use long *a*
and long *o* words.

Sheet, teacher, field, and *money* have the long *e* sound.

| sh**ee**t | t**ea**cher | f**ie**ld | mon**ey** |

Write only the words and phrases that have the long *e* sound in the camping trip list.

money	sunscreen	peaches	meat
bread	pieces of rope	clean clothes	sweets
field glasses	matches	sweaters	donkeys
extra eggs	canteens	honey	thread
peanut butter	sleeping bags	handkerchiefs	cookies

Camping Trip List

1. _____   9. _____

2. _____   10. _____

3. _____   11. _____

4. _____   12. _____

5. _____   13. _____

6. _____   14. _____

7. _____   15. _____

8. _____

Notes for Home: Your child identified and wrote words with the long *e* sound.
Home Activity: Together look at the things written on the list. Talk about what the campers might do with each thing.

The long _e_ sound can be spelled _y_ as in _hungry_ or _e_ as in _she_.

Underline the words in each box that have the long _e_ sound. Then rewrite each sentence. Use a word from the box in place of the underlined word or words.

---

1. they   **2.** we   **3.** she   **4.** he

---

5. What did <u>Keesha</u> tell you about the party?

_____

6. <u>Dave and I</u> are planning to go early.

_____

---

7. reply   **8.** tasty   **9.** many

10. funny   **11.** windy   **12.** why

---

13. There were <u>lots of</u> people at the party.

_____

14. All the food was <u>good</u>.

_____

15. Jerry told <u>silly</u> stories.

_____

Notes for Home: Your child identified words with the long _e_ sound. **Home Activity:** Talk with your child about a party that was fun. Name words with the long _e_ sound that you use in your conversation.

The long *i* sound can be spelled *igh* and *y*.

m*igh*t   **m*y***

Write the answer to each clue and underline the letter or letters that stand for the long *i* sound.

light	sight	sky	tight	right
cry	thigh	reply	fry	fly

1. birds do this _____

2. where to see stars _____

3. one of the five senses _____

4. the opposite of *left* _____

5. babies do this when hungry _____

6. a lamp will give you this _____

7. to cook in oil _____

8. part of your leg _____

9. to answer a question _____

10. the opposite of *loose* _____

Notes for Home: Your child wrote words in which the long *i* sound is spelled *igh* or *y*.
Home Activity: Take turns with your child choosing a word from the list on the page and naming a rhyming word.

Name_____

The long *u* sound can be spelled *u*-consonant-*e* or *u*.

fu**se**   **m**u**sic**

Write the word that belongs in each group of words. Then underline the pattern that spells the long *u* sound in the word.

January	united	huge	Utah	amuse
mule	cube	humorous	pupil	cute

1. March, July, December, _____   *u*-consonant-*e*   *u*

2. big, large, tremendous,_____   *u*-consonant-*e*   *u*

3. horse, zebra, donkey, _____   *u*-consonant-*e*   *u*

4. Illinois, Florida, Texas, _____   *u*-consonant-*e*   *u*

5. learner, scholar, student, _____   *u*-consonant-*e*   *u*

6. funny, silly, amusing, _____   *u*-consonant-*e*   *u*

7. rectangle, circle, pyramid, _____   *u*-consonant-*e*   *u*

8. delight, entertain, raise a smile, _____   *u*-consonant-*e*   *u*

9. cuddly, adorable, sweet, _____   *u*-consonant-*e*   *u*

10. joined, together, one, _____   *u*-consonant-*e*   *u*

Notes for Home: Your child wrote words in which the long *u* sound is spelled *u*-consonant-*e* or *u*. **Home Activity:** Take turns with your child choosing a word he or she wrote on the page and giving a descriptive sentence for it.

Name _____

The long *i* sound can be spelled *igh* and *y*.   **tigh**t   **by**

The long *u* sound can be spelled *u*-consonant-*e* and *u*.   f**u**se   h**u**man

Write the words on the elephants in the correct lists.

cube   mute
reply   bright
night   future
my   amuse

cute   menu
sky   humor
sigh   right
uniform

music   fly
apply   use
light

Long *i* Spelled *igh*

1. _____

2. _____

3. _____

4. _____

5. _____

Long *i* Spelled *y*

6. _____

7. _____

8. _____

9. _____

10. _____

Long *u* Spelled *u*-consonant-*e*

11. _____

12. _____

13. _____

14. _____

15. _____

Long *u* Spelled *u*

16. _____

17. _____

18. _____

19. _____

20. _____

Notes for Home: Your child wrote words with the long *i* and long *u* sounds.
Home Activity: Ask your child to add at least one more word to each list.

Name_____

The letters *a, e, i, o,* and *u* stand for short vowel sounds.

bat   bed   sit   hot   cut

Say each picture name. Write **Yes** if the word has a short vowel sound. Then write the letter that stands for the short vowel sound. Write **No** if the word does not have a short vowel sound.

1.

2.

_____   _____   _____   _____

3.

4.

_____   _____   _____   _____

5.

6.

_____   _____   _____   _____

7.

8.

_____   _____   _____   _____

9.

10.

_____   _____   _____   _____

 Notes for Home: Your child identified words with short vowel sounds.
Home Activity: Have your child cut out magazine pictures whose names have short vowel sounds, paste the pictures on paper, and write the letters that stand for the short vowel sounds in the picture names.

Name_____

Some words have short vowel sounds.

a	**e**	**i**	**o**	**u**
hat	ten	dish	hot	cup

Write the word that answers the question. Underline the letter that stands for the short vowel sound in the word.

1. If you were hot, would you use a jet, a mop, or a fan

   to get cool?   _____

2. Does a mitt, a hand, or a lid cover a pot?   _____

3. Would you wear a cap, a vest, or a muff on your head?   _____

4. Would you ride on a bat, a bus, or a box?   _____

5. What would you use to clean up a spill—a rug, a mitt,

   or a mop?   _____

6. Would you see a sled, a shell, or a bib on a turtle?   _____

7. Can a bat, a pig, or a pup fly?   _____

8. Is a cat, a hen, or a fox a bird?   _____

9. Would a cup, a cut, or a cot need a bandage?   _____

10. Would you swim, run, or hop across a pond?   _____

Notes for Home: Your child identified and wrote words with short vowel sounds.
Home Activity: Take turns with your child asking questions like those on the page. Use words with short vowel sounds as choices for the answers.

A compound word is made up of two words.

air + plane = airplane

Draw lines to match words that make compound words. Write the compound words.

1. foot   coat   _____

2. rain   corn   _____

3. pop   ball   _____

4. hand   ring   _____

5. ear   stand   _____

6. bird   house   _____

7. gold   paper   _____

8. paint   stick   _____

9. drum   brush   _____

10. news   fish   _____

Notes for Home: Your child joined words to make and write compound words.
Home Activity: Write each small word on the page on a piece of scrap paper. Have your child match the papers to form compound words.

A compound word is made of two smaller words.

        when + ever = whenever   left + over = leftover

Underline the compound word that completes the sentence. Then draw a line between the words that make up the compound word.

1. One spring morning after ___,   sunset
   Mom called to me.   breakfast

2. She said we could plant some ___   raindrops
   in the garden.   sunflowers

3. We went ___ into the backyard   outside
   where we have a garden.   inside

4. ___ she turned over some dirt with   However
   a shovel, I saw worms.   Whenever

5. ___ I had to pull up some big   Sometimes
   clumps of weeds.   Anytime

6. Sparrows peeked out of the ___   bedroom
   and watched us dig.   birdhouse

7. We knew that in time ___ beautiful   someone
   would grow.   something

8. We sprinkled seeds on the soil, and then we pushed   into
   the seeds ___ the soil with a rake.   onto

9. As a last step, we poured some ___   buttermilk
   over the soil.   rainwater

10. In the ___, we spend a lot of time   wintertime
    working in our garden.   summertime

Notes for Home: Your child identified the words that make up compound words.
Home Activity: Have your child continue the story by telling what happened after the sunflowers grew. Point out any compound words your child uses.

The letters *igh* and *y* stand for the long *i* sound in *tight* and *cry*.

Follow each direction.

1. Write **fly.** Circle the letter that spells the long *i* sound.   _____

2. Change **f** to **s.** Write the new word.   _____

3. Change **l** to **k.** Write the new word.   _____

4. Change **k** to **h.** Write the new word.   _____

5. Change **s** to **w.** Write the new word.   _____

_____

6. Write **sigh.** Circle the letters that spell the long *i* sound.   _____

7. Add a **t** at the end. Write the new word.   _____

8. Change **s** to **t.** Write the new word.   _____

9. Change the first **t** to **n.** Write the new word.   _____

10. Add a **k** at the beginning. Write the new word.   _____

Notes for Home: Your child wrote words with the long *i* sound spelled *igh* or *y*.
Home Activity: Starting with the word *cry* or *light*, help your child change, add, or subtract letters to make new words.

Name _____

The long *u* sound can be spelled *u*-consonant-*e* or *u*.

cute   unit

Denzel has to find all the words with long *u* spelled *u*-consonant-*e*. Maria has to find all the words with long *u* spelled *u*. Write the words in the correct lists. Not all the words will be used.

music	humor	use	future	mule
sum	amuse	pull	cube	cuteness
fuse	uniform	useful	menu	pupil
number	put	curl	push	burn
must	bush	human	huge	turtle

Denzel's List   **Maria's List**

1. _____   9. _____

2. _____   10. _____

3. _____   11. _____

4. _____   12. _____

5. _____   13. _____

6. _____   14. _____

7. _____   15. _____

8. _____

Notes for Home: Your child wrote words in which the long *u* sound is spelled *u*-consonant-*e* or *u*. **Home Activity:** Take turns with your child choosing a word from each list and making up an oral sentence for it.

29

Name_____

The long *i* sound can be spelled *igh* and *y*.   **righ**t   fl**y**

The long *u* sound can be spelled *u*-consonant-*e* and *u*.   **use**   men**u**

Write *i* or *u* to tell what long vowel sound you hear in each word. Then circle the pattern that spells the long vowel sound.

<u>Word</u>	<u>Vowel Sound Heard</u>	<u>How Is It Spelled?</u>			
1. mule	_____	*igh*	*y*	*u*-consonant-*e*	*u*
2. apply	_____	*igh*	*y*	*u*-consonant-*e*	*u*
3. high	_____	*igh*	*y*	*u*-consonant-*e*	*u*
4. flying	_____	*igh*	*y*	*u*-consonant-*e*	*u*
5. music	_____	*igh*	*y*	*u*-consonant-*e*	*u*
6. tighter	_____	*igh*	*y*	*u*-consonant-*e*	*u*
7. unit	_____	*igh*	*y*	*u*-consonant-*e*	*u*
8. cube	_____	*igh*	*y*	*u*-consonant-*e*	*u*
9. myself	_____	*igh*	*y*	*u*-consonant-*e*	*u*
10. amuse	_____	*igh*	*y*	*u*-consonant-*e*	*u*

Notes for Home: Your child identified the spelling patterns in long *i* and long *u* words.
Home Activity: Help your child list other long *i* and long *u* words. Ask your child what long vowel sound is heard in each word.

The letters *oo* stand for the vowel sounds in these words.

boo**t**   **g**oo**d**

Write each word under the word that has the same vowel sound.

book	foot	hoot	hood	zoo
moon	spoon	hook	broom	wood

soon   **look**

1. _____   6. _____

2. _____   7. _____

3. _____   8. _____

4. _____   9. _____

5. _____   10. _____

Write a word from above that answers each clue.

11. Eat soup with this.   _____

12. Catch fish on this.   _____

13. Owls do this.   _____

14. Sweep the floor with this.   _____

15. A jacket might have this.   _____

Notes for Home: Your child sorted words that have two vowel sounds spelled *oo*.
Home Activity: Have your child read the lists of words under *soon* and *look* and add more words to each list.

The letters _oo_ stand for the vowel sound in _look_.
The letters _oo_ also stand for the vowel sound in _too_.

Unscramble the letters to make words from the list. Write the letters on the lines.
Underline the word at the right that has the same vowel sound as the word you made.

hook	fool	moon	boot	good
wood	goose	hood	school	

1. oogse $\underset{1}{\_\_}$ __ __ __ __   look   cool

2. koco $\underset{2}{\_\_}$ __ __ __   hook   zoo

3. ohod $\underset{3}{\_\_}$ __ __ __   cookie   spool

4. tboo $\underset{4}{\_\_}$ __ __ __   brook   loose

5. oodw $\underset{5}{\_\_}$ __ __ __   took   noodle

6. cosolh   __ __ __ __ $\underset{6}{\_\_}$ __   shook   pool

7. borom $\underset{7}{\_\_}$ __ __ __ __   wool   room

8. ogdo $\underset{8}{\_\_}$ $\underset{9}{\_\_}$ __ __   book   noon

9. nomo $\underset{10}{\_\_}$ __ __ __   stood   balloon

Write the numbered letters to answer the riddle.

Where is a place to learn?

10. __ __ __ __ __ __ __ __ __ __
  1   2   3   4   5   6   7   8   9   10

Notes for Home: Your child identified words with the _oo_ vowel pattern.
Home Activity: List some other words with _oo_. Take turns with your child scrambling the words and having the other person write them correctly.

In *book*, the vowel sound is spelled *oo*.
In *noon*, the vowel sound is spelled *oo*.

Underline the word that has the same vowel sound as the picture name.

1. food   good

2. too   look

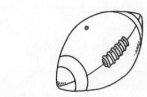

3. boot   wood

4. tool   hood

5. noon   good-bye

6. school   foot

7. cool   brook

8. soon   took

9. pool   stood

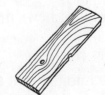

10. broom   cook

Notes for Home: Your child identified the vowel sounds in words with the *oo* pattern.
Home Activity: Have your child choose two words from the page and make up a silly
sentence for them.

33

A compound word is made from two smaller words.

back + yard = backyard   any + body = anybody

Underline two words in each sentence that can be put together to make a compound word. Write the word.

1. I went up to the second floor using the stairs.   _____

2. For a trip in space, you will need a ship.   _____

3. He went out and played along the side of the house.   _____

4. She bought some toys but not another thing.   _____

5. The air in the plane was hot and stuffy.   _____

6. The bed in her room had not been made.   _____

7. A bright moon gave us light to see by.   _____

8. Did you see the sun as it set last evening?   _____

9. There was a lot of news in today's paper.   _____

10. Put the baby into the seat and fasten the belt.   _____

Notes for Home: Your child combined words to make compound words.
Home Activity: Take turns with your child writing the first part of a compound word on a piece of paper and having the other person write the second part of the compound word.

Name _____

A compound word is made up of two words put together.

in + to = into   any + body = anybody

Draw lines to match words to make compound words. Then write the compound words under the heading that tells about them.

1. foot   plane   6. rail   ground

2. out   ball   7. basket   ball

3. air   yard   8. play   ship

4. pop   side   9. space   berries

5. back   corn   10. straw   road

Sports   **Food**

11. _____   13. _____

12. _____   14. _____

Places   **Ways to Travel**

15. _____   18. _____

16. _____   19. _____

17. _____   20. _____

Notes for Home: Your child formed and classified compound words.
Home Activity: Together name other compound words. Think of a category name for each compound.

35

The letters *ou* stand for the vowel sounds in these words.

cloud	**couple**	**boulder**	**would**	**soup**

Write an *ou* word from the box that rhymes with the underlined word.

double	you	ground	touch	group
house	should	shoulder	could	pounce

1. See what I <u>found</u> lying on the _____.

2. Did you see a <u>mouse</u> in the basement of your _____?

3. I hope you made enough <u>soup</u> to feed the whole _____.

4. Each time the ball would <u>bounce</u>, the cat would _____.

5. If you water the plant too <u>much</u>, it will be too wet to _____.

6. If I had a saw, I _____ cut this great big piece of <u>wood</u>.

7. I cannot come to visit _____ because today I have the <u>flu</u>.

8. They moved the <u>boulder</u> off the road and onto the _____.

9. Whenever Dave is in <u>trouble</u>, he wishes he had a _____.

10. To keep my ears warm, I _____ pull up my jacket <u>hood</u>.

Notes for Home: Your child identified words with the *ou* vowel pattern.
Home Activity: Have your child look in a newspaper, find *ou* words, and name rhyming words.

The letters *ou* stand for the vowel sounds in these words.

| cloud | touch | boulder | would | you |

Write each word in the box under the word that has the same vowel sound for *ou*.

should	young	could	shoulder	house
mouse	shout	country	soup	couple
double	group	loud	trouble	ground

ou as in *cloud*   ### *ou* as in *touch*

1. _____   6. _____

2. _____   7. _____

3. _____   8. _____

4. _____   9. _____

5. _____   10. _____

ou as in *would*   ### *ou* as in *you*

11. _____   13. _____

12. _____   14. _____

ou as in *boulder*

15. _____

Notes for Home: Your child grouped words according to their vowel sounds spelled *ou*.
Home Activity: Choose a word from the box and use it to begin a story. Ask your child to choose other words and use them to add to the story.

Name_____   **Digraph *ou* and Diphthong *ou***

The letters *ou* stand for the vowel sounds in these words.

gr**ou**nd   sh**ou**ld   **you**   d**ou**ble   b**ou**lder

Write each word next to a word that has the same vowel sound.

---

about   you   could

1. would _____

2. youth _____

3. sound _____

---

mouse   soup   poultry

4. ground _____

5. shoulder _____

6. toucan _____

---

should   couple

7. young _____

8. could _____

---

trouble   cloud

9. about _____

10. touch _____

Notes for Home: Your child wrote words with the *ou* vowel pattern.
Home Activity: Take turns with your child choosing two words from one of the boxes and making up a sentence with the two words.

38

Name_____

The letters *oo* stand for the vowel sounds in *spoon* and *foot*.

Write each word in the box under the picture whose name has the same vowel sound as the word.

tooth	look	wood	moose	loop
hood	boot	moon	school	took
spool	cook	hook	book	stool
stood	shook	good	goose	zoo

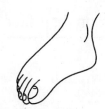

1. _____

2. _____

3. _____

4. _____

5. _____

6. _____

7. _____

8. _____

9. _____

10. _____

11. _____

12. _____

13. _____

14. _____

15. _____

16. _____

17. _____

18. _____

19. _____

20. _____

Notes for Home: Your child sorted *oo* words according to their vowel sounds.
Home Activity: Take turns with your child scrambling words from the lists and writing them correctly.

Name_____

The letters *oo* stand for the vowel sounds in *room* and *foot*.

Underline the words that have the same vowel sound as the word in dark type. Then write the underlined word that goes with each clue.

1. moon   **2.** boots   **3.** look   **4.** stood   **5.** school

room

6. shook   **7.** wood   **8.** shoots   **9.** tools   **10.** took

11. what cowhands wear on their feet   _____

12. a hammer, saw, and wrench   _____

13. something seen in the night sky   _____

14. what a player does with a basketball   _____

15. a place where children learn   _____

16. choose   **17.** mood   **18.** foot   **19.** wood   **20.** loose

took

21. hook   **22.** soon   **23.** books   **24.** moose   **25.** hood

26. a place to hang a coat   _____

27. what some furniture is made of   _____

28. something on a jacket   _____

29. something at the end of a leg   _____

30. what you would see in a library   _____

Notes for Home: Your child wrote words with the *oo* vowel pattern. **Home Activity:** Take turns with your child choosing a word from a list and naming words that rhyme with it.

The letter *j* stands for /j/ in *just*.
The letter *g* stands for /j/ in *gem*.

Underline the word in each sentence that has /j/. Circle the letter that spells /j/.

1. Did you read that page?   j   g

2. Giraffes have long necks.   j   g

3. A kangaroo can jump.   j   g

4. A jungle has many trees.   j   g

5. Do you enjoy singing?   j   g

6. Be gentle with pets.   j   g

7. Read about a giant in a story.   j   g

8. The first month is January.   j   g

9. Let's study about Jupiter.   j   g

10. They have a large cat.   j   g

Notes for Home: Your child identified words in which /j/ is spelled *j* or *g*.
Home Activity: Ask your child to make a sentence in which one word has /j/ spelled *j* or *g*.

The letter *s* stands for /s/ in *safe*.
The letter *c* stands for /s/ in *ice*.

Read each word. Circle **Yes** if you hear /s/. Circle **No** if you do not.

1. city	**2.** side	**3.** can
Yes No	Yes No	Yes No
4. some	**5.** face	**6.** does
Yes No	Yes No	Yes No
7. mice	**8.** call	**9.** once
Yes No	Yes No	Yes No
10. please	**11.** center	**12.** bus
Yes No	Yes No	Yes No
13. cent	**14.** summer	**15.** place
Yes No	Yes No	Yes No

Notes for Home: Your child identified words with /s/ spelled *s* and *c*.
Home Activity: Work together to make your own game like the one on the page. Think of new words. Take turns circling Yes and No.

Name _____

The letters *j* and *g* can spell the *j* sound.   **jump**   **giant**
The letters *s* and *c* can spell the *s* sound.   side   ri**ce**

Underline the words in the box that have /j/ spelled *j* or *g* or that have /s/ spelled *s* or *c*. Write the words you underline in ABC order.

1. joy	**2.** giraffe	**3.** page	**4.** goat	**5.** base
6. ice	**7.** cook	**8.** sent	**9.** gentle	**10.** jeep
11. was	**12.** race	**13.** cup	**14.** mice	**15.** gem
16. some	**17.** edge	**18.** cat	**19.** safe	**20.** city

ABC Order

21. _____   29. _____

22. _____   30. _____

23. _____   31. _____

24. _____   32. _____

25. _____   33. _____

26. _____   34. _____

27. _____   35. _____

28. _____

Notes for Home: Your child identified words in which *j* or *g* spelled /j/ and *s* or *c* spelled /s/.
Home Activity: Have your child choose three words with /j/ and /s/ from a book or magazine and write the words in ABC order.

43

The letters *ai* and *ay* can spell the long *a* sound.

hai**l**   **d**ay

Write *ai* or *ay* to make the words in the list.

tray   mail   train   May
stay   brain   rain   away

1. r _____ _____ n   **2.** aw _____ _____

3. br _____ _____ n   **4.** tr _____ _____ n

5. st _____ _____   **6.** M _____ _____

7. m _____ _____ l   **8.** tr _____ _____

Write a word from above that answers each clue.

9. This is wet and falls in drops.   **10.** An engine and cars make up this.

_____   _____

11. If you do not leave, you do this.   **12.** This is the month after April.

_____   _____

13. A package might be called this.   **14.** You carry things on this.

_____   _____

15. You think with this.

_____

Notes for Home: Your child identified and wrote words with long *a* spelled *ai* and *ay*.
Home Activity: Have your child find and circle words in a newspaper in which long *a* is
spelled *ai* or *ay*.

Name_____

The letters *oa, ow,* and *o* stand for the long *o* sound.

boat   show   most

Put each sentence in the correct order. Circle two words with the long *o* sound.

1. The old is radio. _____

2. wore a coat one No. _____

3. this down Go road. _____

4. soap Does the float? _____

5. throat My is sore so. _____

6. coach is hero The a. _____

7. a toad a song Can croak? _____

8. is mowed The lawn almost.

_____

9. along the coast walked slowly We.

_____

10. poem The does not about snow rhyme.

_____

Notes for Home: Your child identified words with the long *o* sound spelled *oa, ow,* and *o*. **Home Activity:** Have your child make up other sentences that have at least one word with the long *o* sound.

45

Name_____

The letters *ow* stand for the vowel sounds in these words.

grow   **how**

Write words from the box to complete the phrases.

down	throw	window	now	town
snow	below	shower	slow	frown

1. not up, but _____

2. not door, but_____

3. not above, but _____

4. not catch, but _____

5. not later, but _____

6. not rain, but _____

7. not fast, but _____

8. not bath, but _____

9. not smile, but _____

10. not city, but _____

Write each word in the box under the word that has the same vowel sound.

grow   **clown**

11. _____

16. _____

12. _____

17. _____

13. _____

18. _____

14. _____

19. _____

15. _____

20. _____

Notes for Home: Your child wrote words with the *ow* vowel pattern.
Home Activity: Take turns with your child naming a word on the page and then pointing to and naming another word on the page with the same vowel sound.

Name_____ **Digraph *ow* and Diphthong *ow***

The letters *ow* stand for the vowel sounds in *grow* and *how*.

Write the word that goes with the picture. Circle the letters that stand for the vowel sound in *grow* or *how*.

clown   shower   crowd   crown   arrow
row   shadow   howl   crow   pillow

1.  _____

2.  _____

3. _____

4. _____

5.  _____

6. _____

7. _____

8. _____

9.  _____

10.  _____

Notes for Home: Your child identified and wrote words with the *ow* vowel pattern.
Home Activity: You and your child draw a picture of something whose name has the letters *ow*. Name each other's picture and then name another word with the same vowel sound.

47

Name_____

The letters *ow* stand for the vowel sounds in these words.

cl**ow**n   be**low**

Follow the directions. Write the new words. Then circle the answer to the question.

1. blow   Change **bl** to **gr.**   _____

              Change **gr** to **cr.**   _____

Does *ow* stand for the same sound in each word you wrote?   Yes   No

2. row   Change **r** to **sn.**   _____

              Change **sn** to **pl.**   _____

Does *ow* stand for the same sound in each word you wrote?   Yes   No

3. know   Change **kn** to **m.**   _____

              Change **m** to **c.**   _____

Does *ow* stand for the same sound in each word you wrote?   Yes   No

4. power   Change **p** to **t.**   _____

              Change **t** to **fl.**   _____

Does *ow* stand for the same sound in each word you wrote?   Yes   No

5. yellow   Change **ye** to **a.**   _____

              Change **al** to **be.**   _____

Does *ow* stand for the same sound in each word you wrote?   Yes   No

Notes for Home: Your child wrote words with the *ow* vowel pattern.
Home Activity: Starting with *down, snow,* or *crown,* help your child change letters to make new words.

The letters *j* and *g* can stand for /j/.   **just**   **age**

In each category, write the words that have the *j* sound spelled *j* or *g*.

<table>
<tr><td>

Months

January **1.** _____

June   **2.** _____

July   **3.** _____

August

</td><td>

Clothes

jacket   **4.** _____

jumper   **5.** _____

gloves   **6.** _____

jeans

</td></tr>
<tr><td>

Size

huge   **7.** _____

big   **8.** _____

jumbo   **9.** _____

large

</td><td>

Names

Ginger   **10.** _____

Greg   **11.** _____

Joel   **12.** _____

George

</td></tr>
</table>

Places

garden **13.** _____

Japan   **14.** _____

region **15.** _____

village

Notes for Home: Your child wrote words in which /j/ is spelled *j* or *g*.
Home Activity: Take turns with your child naming another word that belongs in each group and telling whether the word has /j/ spelled *j* or *g*.

The letters *s* and *c* can stand for /s/. **saw** **race**

Write the word that answers each clue. Circle the letter that stands for the *s* sound.

| city | summer | mice | pencil | baseball |
| yes | sea | ceiling | cereal | soft |

1. the top of a room _____ s c

2. a season of the year _____ s c

3. place where many people live _____ s c

4. the opposite of *no* _____ s c

5. something to write with _____ s c

6. a large body of water _____ s c

7. more than one mouse _____ s c

8. something to eat in the morning _____ s c

9. the opposite of *hard* _____ s c

10. a sport with a batter _____ s c

Notes for Home: Your child wrote words in which /s/ is spelled *s* or *c*.
Home Activity: Ask your child to think of other words that have /s/ spelled *s* or *c* and to make up meaning clues for the words.

Name_____

In some pairs of letters, only one letter stands for a sound. The other letter is silent. Note the silent letter in each of these words.

wrench   **kn**ob   fas**t**en   desi**gn**   cli**mb**

Write the letter that is not heard in each word.

1. wren _____   **2.** knot _____

3. knew _____   **4.** lamb _____

5. sign _____   **6.** wrap _____

7. wrong _____   **8.** assign _____

9. comb _____   **10.** listen _____

Write the word that completes each sentence. Use words from above.

11. Mary had a little _____.

12. She _____ it could not go to school with her.

13. It was _____ for her pet to follow her.

14. She read the _____ that said, "No pets at school!"

15. But the animal would not _____ to her and stay at home.

Notes for Home: Your child identified words with silent letters. **Home Activity:** Have your child read sentences on the page. Discuss how Mary could solve her problem.

Name _____

Each of these words has a silent letter—a letter that does not stand for a sound.

wrap   **kn**ot   fas**t**en   desi**gn**   com**b**

Write a rhyming word for each numbered word below.

write	sign	wreath	lamb	knuckle
knee	knit	thumb	reign	listen

1. fit _____

2. some _____

3. night _____

4. tree _____

5. mine _____

6. train _____

7. ham _____

8. buckle _____

9. teeth _____

10. glisten _____

Use the words you wrote above to answer these questions.

11. Which two words have a silent *w*?

_____ _____

12. Which three words have a silent *k*?

_____ _____ _____

13. Which word has a silent *t*? _____

14. Which two words have a silent *g*?

_____ _____

15. Which two words have a silent *b*?

_____ _____

Notes for Home: Your child identified silent letters in words. **Home Activity:** Have your child look through newspaper and magazine ads for other words with silent letters and then circle each word and tell what letter is silent.

52

Name_____

The letters *ou* stand for the vowel sounds in these words.

gro*u*nd   **sh*ou*ld**   **y*ou***   **t*ou*ch**   **p*ou*ltry**

Write each word on the line with the matching number. Then underline the word that rhymes with the word you wrote.

(5) soup   **(1)** double   **(9)** mouth   **(10)** shout   **(8)** shoulder
(2) boulder   **(4)** would   **(6)** cloud   **(3)** round   **(7)** pouch

1. _____   grouch   would   trouble

2. _____   shoulder   younger   prouder

3. _____   proud   pound   doubled

4. _____   sound   counted   could

5. _____   shout   bounce   group

6. _____   crowd   should   roughed

7. _____   though   young   couch

8. _____   boulder   counter   tougher

9. _____   fourth   south   count

10. _____   southern   about   thought

Notes for Home: Your child wrote words with the *ou* vowel pattern.
Home Activity: Take turns with your child choosing a word that was not underlined and giving a rhyming word.

Name_____

Listen to the different sounds the letters *ou* can stand for.

so**und**   **c**o**uld**   **y**o**u**   **c**o**uple**   **sh**o**ulder**

Put an X on the box if the letters *ou* stand for two different vowel sounds in the words.

1. about around H	**2.** should would W	**3.** toucan scout G
4. double country O	**5.** proud youth R	**6.** you soup A
7. mouth group E	**8.** touch young F	**9.** loud noun I
10. house pound R	**11.** amount trouble A	**12.** poultry boulder L
13. would found T	**14.** cougar group H	**15.** double young D

Write the letters from the boxes with X's. There is a message for you.

_____ _____ _____ _____ _____!

Notes for Home: Your child identified words with the *ou* vowel pattern.
Home Activity: With your child, change one word in a box that has an X. Make both words have the same vowel sound for *ou*.

Name _____

In each of these words, the letters *ou* stand for a different vowel sound.

ar**ou**nd   c**ou**ld   y**ou**   t**ou**ch   sh**ou**lder

Change the words to make new words with the *ou* vowel pattern. Add and subtract letters. Write each new word.

1. mouse – se + th =   _____

2. group – gr + s =   _____

3. should – ld + t =   _____

4. pouch – ch + nd =   _____

5. young – ng + th =   _____

6. couch – ch + ld =   _____

7. fountain – f + m =   _____

8. boulder – b + sh =   _____

9. toucan – an + h =   _____

10. could – ld + nt =   _____

Notes for Home: Your child wrote words with the *ou* vowel pattern.
Home Activity: Together write some words that have *ou* in them and make new words by subtracting and adding letters.

The letters *ar* and *or* stand for the vowel sounds in these words.

f*ar*m   **h*or*n**

Underline the word that has the same vowel sound as the picture name.

1.

cart   cord

2.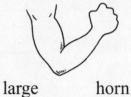

large   horn

3.

dark   orbit

4.

far   store

5.

farm   north

6.

card   story

7.

yard   force

8.

park   short

9.

bark   more

10.

part   fort

Notes for Home: Your child identified words with the *ar* and *or* vowel sounds.
Home Activity: Have your child look through magazines for pictures of things whose names
have the *ar* or *or* vowel sound.

The letters *er, ir, or,* and *ur* stand for the vowel sound in these words.

he**r**	**b**i**r**d	**w**o**r**d	**f**ur

Write the word in the sentence that has the vowel sound in *her, bird, word,* and *fur.*
Circle the letters that stand for the vowel sound.

1. A fern is a plant. _____ er   ir
              or   ur

2. I have a burn on my hand. _____ er   ir
              or   ur

3. Turtles walk slowly. _____ er   ir
              or   ur

4. She won third prize. _____ er   ir
              or   ur

5. Draw a circle on the sidewalk. _____ er   ir
              or   ur

6. The poem has two verses. _____ er   ir
              or   ur

7. Here is a world map. _____ er   ir
              or   ur

8. I want to be a nurse. _____ er   ir
              or   ur

9. The skirt touched the ground. _____ er   ir
              or   ur

10. A worm is on the sidewalk. _____ er   ir
              or   ur

Notes for Home: Your child identified words with the *er, ir, or,* and *ur* vowel patterns.
Home Activity: Take turns with your child choosing a word written above. One person writes
the word, leaving out two letters. The other person guesses the word and writes the missing
letters.

The letters *air* and *are* stand for the vowel sound in these words.   h**air**   c**are**

The letters *ear* stand for the vowel sound in this word.   h**ear**

Write each word in the box that has a word with the same vowel sound and the same spelling.

pair	scare	clear	fear	hare
fair	dare	parent	flair	gear
near	air	dear	careful	stair

hair

1. _____

2. _____

3. _____

4. _____

5. _____

care

6. _____

7. _____

8. _____

9. _____

10. _____

hear

11. _____

12. _____

13. _____

14. _____

15. _____

Notes for Home: Your child identified words with the *air, are,* and *ear* vowel patterns.
Home Activity: Choose two words, each from a different box. Make up a sentence with them. Then have your child take a turn doing the same thing.

The letters *ow* stand for the vowel sounds in *own* and *down*.

Draw a line from the word in the box to the word with the same vowel sound.

1. | now |

grow
growl
own

2. | owe |

show
scowl
power

3. | town |

low
mow
brown

4. | bowl |

vowel
cow
owner

5. | crow |

crowd
tower
flow

6. | shower |

throw
now
snow

7. | powder |

plow
mower
blow

8. | slow |

own
frown
powder

9. | tow |

flower
how
glow

10. | crown |

allow
stow
below

Notes for Home: Your child matched words with the same vowel sound spelled *ow*.
Home Activity: With one hand, point to a word on the page. With the other hand, point to another word with the same vowel sound. Then ask your child to take a turn.

Name _____

The letters *ow* stand for the vowel sounds in *down* and *own*.

Write a word from the box that has the same vowel sound as the underlined word
and completes the sentence.

town	slowly	grow	bowling	mow
growling	vowel	throw	flower	towel

1. I <u>know</u> it is time for me to _____ the grass.

2. A large <u>crowd</u> gathered in the _____ square.

3. The <u>clown</u> had a _____ that squirted water.

4. I would like to <u>own</u> a red _____ ball.

5. The <u>snowman</u> _____ melted in the warm sun.

6. After my <u>shower</u>, I dried off with a _____.

7. The man <u>scowled</u> at the _____ dog.

8. Will you <u>show</u> me how to _____ a football?

9. The <u>row</u> of corn started to _____ tall.

10. <u>Somehow</u> I will learn all the _____ sounds.

Notes for Home: Your child wrote words with the *ow* vowel pattern.
Home Activity: Read two words from the box. Have your child tell if the two words have the
same vowel sound. Then let your child read two words.

To find the base word, you must take off any prefixes, suffixes, or endings.

uncover   care**ful**   **search**es   re**build**ing

Add the prefixes, suffixes, or endings to the base words. Write the new word.

1. re + teach = _____

2. pull + ing = _____

3. re + fold + ed = _____

4. dis + honest + ly = _____

5. help + less + ness = _____

Write the base word for each word.

6. remake

_____

7. played

_____

8. dislike

_____

9. unsafe

_____

10. cheerful

_____

11. stamping

_____

12. unpacked

_____

13. unfairness

_____

14. incorrectly

_____

15. replacement

_____

Notes for Home: Your child identified base words. **Home Activity:** Take turns with your child writing the words 6–15 as word equations like the examples in 1–5. Use plus and equal signs.

61

Sometimes the spelling of base words is changed when a suffix or ending is added.

The final *e* is dropped.	take	tak**ing**
The final consonant is doubled.	sit	sit**ting**
The final *y* is changed to *i*.	happy	happ**iness**

Write 1, 2, or 3 to show what happened to each base word. Then write the base word.

1. The final *e* was dropped.
2. The final consonant was doubled.
3. The final *y* was changed to *i*.

1. stopped _____   **2.** riding _____

_____   _____

3. babies _____   **4.** waving _____

_____   _____

5. cutting _____   **6.** biggest _____

_____   _____

7. stories _____   **8.** hurried _____

_____   _____

9. approval _____   **10.** driver _____

_____   _____

Notes for Home: Your child identified the changes made to the spelling of base words when suffixes or endings were added. **Home Activity:** Using the base words that were written on the lines, help your child make up an adventure story.

Name_____

Sometimes the spelling of a base word changes when a suffix or an ending is added.

Prefix Added

happy   **un**happy

Final Consonant Doubled

sit   sit**ting**

Final *e* Dropped

drive   driv**er**

Final *y* Changed to *i*

baby   bab**ies**

Write the base word of each word.

1. misplace _____

2. bunnies _____

3. gladness _____

4. lovable _____

5. hidden _____

6. wiggling _____

7. searches _____

8. worried _____

9. happily _____

10. mysterious _____

Write the base word from above that completes each sentence.

11. Our _____ was missing.

12. How could he _____ out of the cage and escape?

13. We _____ him very much and want to find him.

14. Our pet makes us _____.

15. When we saw he was gone, we began to cry and _____.

16. "Let's _____ the yard," said Mother.

17. Our pet _____ himself very well.

18. When we found him, we were very _____.

19. We put him back in his _____ in the cage.

20. The _____ of the missing bunny was solved.

Notes for Home: Your child identified and wrote base words. **Home Activity:** Use the base words written for 1–10 to tell a story together about a family pet or adventure.

The letters *ar, er, ir, or,* and *ur* stand for the vowel sounds in these words.

par**k**   **h**er   sk**ir**t   **horn**   **burn**

Underline 15 words in the paragraph that have a vowel-*r* sound. Then write each word under the heading where it belongs.

When the dog began to bark, we knew something was wrong. Bert and I ran to the yard. We saw the dog digging up dirt by the porch. A large turtle was stuck between two slats. We were certain we could be of service. First we removed some soil in a circle around the animal. In a short time, it was free. It was not hurt, so we returned it to the pond. What a great story we had to tell!

ar as in *far*

1. _____

2. _____

3. _____

er as in *fern*

4. _____

5. _____

6. _____

ir as in *bird*

7. _____

8. _____

9. _____

or as in *fort*

10. _____

11. _____

12. _____

ur as in *turn*

13. _____

14. _____

15. _____

Notes for Home: Your child identified and sorted words with vowel-*r* sounds.
Home Activity: Tell a story about a time you helped someone. Then ask your child to tell a story about a time he or she helped someone.

The letters *air, are, ear,* and *or* stand for the vowel sounds in these words.

chair   **c**a**re**   **d**ear   **w**or**d**

Write the word from the box that goes with the meaning. Then circle the letters that stand for the vowel sound.

glare	clear	worst	hare	scare
near	world	pair	hear	hair

1. to frighten   _____

2. what covers your head   _____

3. two of a kind   _____

4. not cloudy   _____

5. an angry look   _____

6. another name for the Earth   _____

7. the opposite of *best*   _____

8. close to   _____

9. a kind of rabbit   _____

10. to listen to   _____

Notes for Home: Your child matched vowel-*r* words with meaning clues.
Home Activity: Make up a sentence for a word in the box. Have your child identify the word with the vowel-*r* sound. Continue until all the words are used.

Name _____

A suffix is added to the end of a word.

dark + ness = dark**ness**   silent + ly = silent**ly**

arm + ful = arm**ful**   humor + ous = humor**ous**

Circle the suffix that can be added to the base word to make a new word. Then write the new word.

Word	Suffixes		New Word
1. care	ly	ful	_____
2. great	ness	ous	_____
3. final	ly	ous	_____
4. danger	ness	ous	_____
5. late	ly	ful	_____
6. joy	ous	ness	_____
7. kind	ness	ful	_____
8. near	ly	ous	_____
9. rest	ous	ful	_____
10. sad	ness	ful	_____
11. hope	ly	ful	_____
12. soft	ous	ness	_____
13. forget	ness	ful	_____
14. quick	ly	ous	_____
15. vigor	ous	ness	_____

Notes for Home: Your child added suffixes to base words to make new words.
Home Activity: Have your child find words with suffixes in newspaper ads and tell what suffix was added to each word.

Name _____

When suffixes are added to words, they change the meaning of the words.

ness = a state of being ___	dark**ness** = a state of being dark
ly = in a ___ way	loud**ly** = in a loud way
ful = full of	hope**ful** = full of hope
ous = having ___	humor**ous** = having humor

Write the word for each meaning clue. Use the underlined word and one of these suffixes: *-ness, -ly, -ful, -ous.*

1. a state of being <u>quick</u>

_____

2. full of <u>hope</u>

_____

3. in a <u>soft</u> way

_____

4. having <u>joy</u>

_____

5. full of <u>power</u>

_____

6. in a <u>brave</u> way

_____

7. having <u>danger</u>

_____

8. a state of being <u>ill</u>

_____

9. a state of being <u>sad</u>

_____

10. full of <u>peace</u>

_____

11. in a <u>neat</u> way

_____

12. having <u>glamor</u>

_____

13. full of <u>use</u>

_____

14. a state of being <u>polite</u>

_____

15. in a <u>swift</u> way

_____

Notes for Home: Your child used meaning clues and suffixes to make new words.
Home Activity: Take turns with your child using words that were written on the page to make up sentences about famous people.

Sometimes the spelling of a base word changes before a suffix is added.

happy – y + i + ness = happiness

Add the suffix to each base word. Write the new word.

1. merry + ly = _____

2. mystery + ous = _____

3. happy + ly = _____

4. fury + ous = _____

5. crunchy + ness = _____

6. victory + ous = _____

7. empty + ness = _____

8. greedy + ness = _____

9. beauty + ful = _____

10. melody + ous = _____

11. easy + ly = _____

12. pretty + ness = _____

13. bumpy + ness = _____

14. angry + ly = _____

15. glory + ous = _____

Notes for Home: Your child changed the spelling of base words before adding suffixes.
Home Activity: Have your child add suffixes to the words *lazy, hungry,* and *busy* and tell how the spelling had to change.

Sometimes words have letters that do not stand for a sound.

    write   **kn**ob   fas**t**en   **gn**at   lim**b**

Circle the word in each pair that has a silent consonant *w, k, t, g,* or *b*. Then write the word in the box where it belongs.

1. quarter	knot	**2.** fox	lamb
3. wrench	went	**4.** listen	hurt
5. kit	knee	**6.** germ	design
7. comb	cub	**8.** water	wreath
9. sign	hard	**10.** glisten	spot

silent *w*	**silent *k***
11. _____	13. _____
12. _____	14. _____

silent *t*	**silent *g***
15. _____	17. _____
16. _____	18. _____

silent *b*
19. _____
20. _____

Notes for Home: Your child identified and sorted words with silent letters.
Home Activity: Take turns with your child choosing a word, drawing a picture of it, and having the other person write the word for the picture.

Name _____

In some letter pairs, one letter is silent.

write   **kn**ot   fas**t**en   **gn**at   crum**b**

Draw lines to match two words with the same silent letter. Then write each word pair and tell what letter is silent.

1. wrap	assign	**6.** comb	wreck
2. limb	glisten	**7.** resign	knock
3. sign	knit	**8.** listener	lamb
4. listen	climb	**9.** wren	design
5. knee	wreath	**10.** know	Christmas

11. The words _____ and _____ have a silent _____.

12. The words _____ and _____ have a silent _____.

13. The words _____ and _____ have a silent _____.

14. The words _____ and _____ have a silent _____.

15. The words _____ and _____ have a silent _____.

16. The words _____ and _____ have a silent _____.

17. The words _____ and _____ have a silent _____.

18. The words _____ and _____ have a silent _____.

19. The words _____ and _____ have a silent _____.

20. The words _____ and _____ have a silent _____.

Notes for Home: Your child identified silent letters in words. **Home Activity:** Take turns with your child making up a silly sentence for each pair of words and telling what letter is silent in the two words.

The letters *th, ch, ph,* and *sh* can sometimes be found in the middle of words. The two letters stand for one sound.

fa**th**er   rea**ch**ed   tele**ph**one   book**sh**elf

Circle the letters that stand for the sound you hear in the middle of each picture name.

1.

th   ch   ph   sh

2.

th   ch   ph   sh

3.

th   ch   ph   sh

4.

th   ch   ph   sh

5.

th   ch   ph   sh

6.

th   ch   ph   sh

7.

th   ch   ph   sh

8.

th   ch   ph   sh

9.

th   ch   ph   sh

10.

th   ch   ph   sh

Notes for Home: Your child identified consonant digraphs in the middle of words.
Home Activity: Have your child choose one of these consonant digraphs: *th, ch, ph, sh.*
Together write all the words you can think of with these letters in the middle.

Name_____

The letters *th, ch, ph,* and *sh* can sometimes be found in the middle of words.

gather   reaches   telephone   fishing

Write the word from the box that answers each clue. Circle the letters *th, ch, ph,* or *sh* that appear in the middle of the word.

peaches	alphabet	trophy	seashells	perches
weather	elephant	beaches	father	bookshelves

1. This animal has a trunk.   _____

2. A dad may be called this.   _____

3. A beach is where these can be found.   _____

4. Rain, snow, and sun are part of this.   _____

5. You might win this as a prize.   _____

6. A library has many of these for books.   _____

7. These feel fuzzy to the touch.   _____

8. These are sandy places.   _____

9. This is another name for the ABC's.   _____

10. These are places for birds to rest.   _____

Notes for Home: Your child wrote words with consonant digraphs in the middle.
Home Activity: Choose a word from the box and make up a clue for it. Ask your child to guess the word. Then have your child choose a word.

Name _____

Sometimes the letters *th, ch, ph,* and *sh* stand for sounds heard in the middle of words.

    any**th**ing   rea**ch**es   tele**ph**one   da**sh**ed

Write *th, ch, ph,* or *sh* to complete a word that makes sense in the sentence.

  1. Look at that big gray ele____ ____ant.

  2. I hope we have sun____ ____ine and not rain today.

  3. Fill the ba____ ____tub with warm water.

  4. Who coa____ ____es your team?

  5. My grandfa____ ____er is coming for a visit.

  6. Consuelo collects sea____ ____ells.

  7. Did you buy any____ ____ing at the store?

  8. My grades are un____ ____anged.

  9. The first-prize winner received a tro____ ____y.

10. Do you know the al____ ____abet song?

11. A crowd ga____ ____ered to watch the parade.

12. I like poa____ ____ed eggs.

13. Please re____ ____eck your work.

14. A go____ ____er dug tunnels under our lawn.

15. Your friend____ ____ip is important to me.

Notes for Home: Your child wrote consonant digraphs in the middle of words.
Home Activity: Take turns with your child writing other words with the letters *th, ch, ph,* or *sh* in the middle, leaving out the letters, and having the other person write the missing letters.

Name _____

A base word is a word without any prefixes, suffixes, or endings added.

	rerun	neighborhood	singing
Base Words:	run	neighbor	sing

Add the prefixes, suffixes, or endings shown to the base word to make new words.

lock

1. un + _____ = _____

2. _____ + ing = _____

3. _____ + er = _____

play

4. re + _____ = _____

5. _____ + ed = _____

6. _____ + er = _____

correct

7. in + _____ = _____

8. _____ + ing = _____

9. _____ + ion = _____

10. in + _____ + ly = _____

Notes for Home: Your child added prefixes, suffixes, and endings to base words.
Home Activity: Take turns with your child choosing a base word, adding a prefix, suffix, or ending, and then using the new word in a sentence.

When suffixes or endings are added to base words, the spelling of the base word sometimes changes.

Drop the final *e*.	come = coming
Double the final consonant.	run = running
Change *y* to *i*.	try = tries
No change	sing = singing

Write each word in the box that shows how the base word was changed.

armful	mysterious	lovable	biggest	worried
location	nearly	librarian	dirtiest	determination
approval	searches	hesitated	hidden	neighborhood
shutting	careful	memories	swimming	beginner

Drop the Final *e*	**Double the Final Consonant**
1. _____	6. _____
2. _____	7. _____
3. _____	8. _____
4. _____	9. _____
5. _____	10. _____
Change *y* to *i*	**No Change**
11. _____	16. _____
12. _____	17. _____
13. _____	18. _____
14. _____	19. _____
15. _____	20. _____

Notes for Home: Your child identified the spelling changes made to base words when suffixes or endings are added. **Home Activity:** Have your child add one more word to each list.

Consonants blends, such as *bl, gl,* and *st,* can stand for the beginning sound in a word.

Circle the blend that stands for the sound at the beginning of each picture name. Then write the blend to complete the word.

1. st
   sp
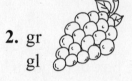

_____ _____ ar

2. gr
   gl

_____ _____ apes

3. pr
   pl

_____ _____ ane

4. fl
   fr

_____ _____ ower

5. dr
   tr

_____ _____ ill

6. fl
   fr

_____ _____ uit

7. sp
   st

_____ _____ ool

8. sm
   sn

_____ _____ ile

9. bl
   br
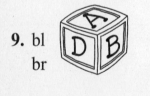

_____ _____ ock

10. gr
   gl

_____ _____ asses

 Notes for Home: Your child identified initial consonant blends in words.
Home Activity: Choose a consonant blend from the page and name two words that begin with the blend. Then have your child choose a blend and name two words for it.

Consonant blends, such as *st, nt,* and *mp,* can stand for the ending sound in a word.

Circle the picture whose name has the ending sound spelled by the consonant blend.

1. nt

2. mp

3. st

4. st

5. nd

6. lt

7. mp

8. sk

9. nt

10. ld

Notes for Home: Your child identified the final consonant blends in words.
Home Activity: Name a word that ends with a consonant blend. Write the letters that stand for the ending sound. Then ask your child to do the same.

Consonant blends can stand for the sound at the beginning of words.
Consonant blends can stand for the sound at the end of words.

Fill in the circle under the blend that begins or ends each picture name.

Beginning

1. fr br tr

2. sn st sp

3. tr gl pr

4. sl sm st

5. bl pl fl

Ending

6. mp nd nt

7. lt nd ld

8. ct lt nt

9. st nt lt

10. st sk nd

Notes for Home: Your child identified initial or final consonant blends in picture names.
Home Activity: With your child, look through a newspaper. Circle words with beginning or
ending blends.

Consonant digraphs, such as *th, ch, ph,* and *sh,* sometimes come in the middle of words. The two letters stand for one sound.

ano**th**er   rea**ch**ing   go**ph**er   fini**sh**ed

Write the word from the list that completes each sentence. Circle the digraph that is found in the middle of the word.

inchworm	father	telephone	feather	trophy
branches	washing	elephant	seashells	bookshelves
teacher	weather	bathtub	mushrooms	alphabet

1. Circus goes with _____.   th   ch   ph   sh

2. Prize goes with _____.   th   ch   ph   sh

3. Moth goes with _____.   th   ch   ph   sh

4. Mother goes with _____.   th   ch   ph   sh

5. School goes with _____.   th   ch   ph   sh

6. Beach goes with _____.   th   ch   ph   sh

7. Tree goes with _____.   th   ch   ph   sh

8. Library goes with _____.   th   ch   ph   sh

9. Rain goes with _____.   th   ch   ph   sh

10. ABC goes with _____.   th   ch   ph   sh

11. Cleaning goes with _____.   th   ch   ph   sh

12. Shower goes with _____.   th   ch   ph   sh

13. Call goes with _____.   th   ch   ph   sh

14. Bird goes with _____.   th   ch   ph   sh

15. Pizza goes with _____.   th   ch   ph   sh

Notes for Home: Your child identified consonant digraphs in the middle of words.
Home Activity: Go through the sentences together. Take turns giving another word that could complete each sentence.

Name _____

Father, inchworm, elephant, and *fishing* all have consonant digraphs in the middle.

Circle the word in each question that has a *th, ch, ph,* or *sh* in the middle. Then use the circled word to write an answer to the question.

1. Where might you see an elephant?

_____

2. What does a flashlight need to work?

_____

3. Where do you put toothpaste?

_____

4. What game do you play with your brother?

_____

5. Where could you find a seashell?

_____

6. What does a teacher do?

_____

7. Who might win a trophy?

_____

8. How do peaches taste?

_____

9. What is the last letter of the alphabet?

_____

10. What could you make in a workshop?

_____

Notes for Home: Your child identified words with medial consonant digraphs.
Home Activity: Choose a circled word from the page and ask a question, using the word in the question. Have your child answer the question.

Some consonant blends, such as *scr, str,* and *spr,* have three letters. They can stand for the beginning sound in a word.

Circle the letters that stand for the beginning sound in the picture name. Add the circled letters to the letters shown to make a new word.

1.   str   spr

___ + eam = _____

2.    spl   spr

___ + ay = _____

3.   scr   spl

___ + een = _____

4.    squ   spl

___ + awk = _____

5.   str   spl

___ + ash = _____

6.   thr   spr

___ + one = _____

7.   scr   spl

___ + eech = _____

8.   spr   str

___ + eet = _____

9.   str   spr

___ + out = _____

10.   spr   thr

___ + oat = _____

 Notes for Home: Your child identified three-letter consonant blends in words.
Home Activity: Look through a favorite storybook with your child. Find words with three-letter blends and tell what three letters begin each word.

Name _____

Consonant blends with three letters, such as *spr, spl,* or *thr,* can come at the beginning of a word. The three letters stand for one sound.

Make new words. Change the underlined letter or letters in each word. Add the three-letter blend. Write the new word.

scr

1. <u>b</u>eam _____

2. <u>b</u>een _____

squ

3. <u>s</u>peak _____

4. <u>s</u>neeze _____

spl

5. <u>w</u>inter _____

6. <u>c</u>rash _____

spr

7. <u>f</u>ling _____

8. <u>tw</u>inkle _____

str

9. <u>s</u>weet _____

10. <u>ch</u>ange _____

thr

11. <u>m</u>ust _____

12. <u>c</u>oat _____

Complete each sentence. Use a word you wrote above.

13. When I am scared, I _____.

14. A mouse might make a _____.

15. The season before summer is _____.

16. I have a sore _____.

17. In a swimming pool, people like to _____.

18. Look both ways when crossing a _____.

19. A hug is a big _____.

20. A window might be covered by a _____.

Notes for Home: Your child wrote words with three-letter blends. **Home Activity:** Take turns with your child pointing to a three-letter blend and naming a word that begins with that blend.

Three-letter blends stand for the beginning sounds in these words.

squeak   **str**eet   **thr**ee

Write the word that answers the question. Circle the blend.

1. Does a mouse **scream** or **squeak?**   _____

2. Is **spring** or **string** a season?   _____

3. Would you **sprig** or **splash** in a bathtub?   _____

4. Are eggs usually **scrambled** or **scraped?**   _____

5. Does a **screw** or a **scrap** hold something together?   _____

6. Would a shirt have **stripes** or **scrunches?**   _____

7. Does a backpack have a **strap** or a **sprain?**   _____

8. Is a **square** or a **scream** a shape?   _____

9. Do you **split** or **strain** wood?   _____

10. Does a **splinter** or a **sprinkler** water a lawn?   _____

11. Is **three** or **through** an age?   _____

12. Might a cat **squeeze** or **scratch** you?   _____

13. Could a **throat** or a **throne** feel sore?   _____

14. Might you **sprout** or **sprain** an ankle?   _____

15. Would you **scrub** or **scratch** a floor to make it clean?   _____

Notes for Home: Your child identified words with three-letter blends.
Home Activity: Have your child use each word he or she wrote in a sentence.

Name_____

A consonant blend can stand for the sound at the beginning or end of a word.

drum	**cl**oud	**sm**all
ha**nd**	a**sk**	co**ld**

Write each word in the box where it belongs. Then write the blend or blends found in the words.

mask	meant	gleam	gold	friend
train	lamp	bend	plate	vest
guest	dry	smile	risk	spider
greed	crust	scout	belt	steam

Beginning Blends	**Ending Blends**
1. _____ _____	10. _____ _____
2. _____ _____	11. _____ _____
3. _____ _____	12. _____ _____
4. _____ _____	13. _____ _____
5. _____ _____	14. _____ _____
6. _____ _____	15. _____ _____
7. _____ _____	16. _____ _____
8. _____ _____	17. _____ _____
9. _____ _____	18. _____ _____

Both Beginning and Ending Blends

19. _____ _____ _____

20. _____ _____ _____

Notes for Home: Your child wrote words with initial and final consonant blends.
Home Activity: Ask your child to choose a word from the page and to name another word with the same beginning or ending blend. Then you take a turn.

Name_____

A consonant blend can stand for the sound at the beginning or end of a word.

drum   **gr**apes   **pl**ate   ha**nd**   ma**sk**   sta**mp**

Circle the blend in each word. Then write the words where they belong in the sentence. Some words will not be used.

      snow   melt   sand

1. The _____ began to _____ in the sun.

      toast   grapes   skates

2. We ate juicy _____ and crunchy _____.

      belt   nest   dress

3. Mom bought a _____ and a _____.

      lamp   plane   cloud

4. I saw a _____ and a _____ in the sky.

      sweep   broom   spoon

5. Get a _____ and _____ the floor.

Notes for Home: Your child wrote words with initial and final consonant blends.
Home Activity: Have your child choose three words from the page and use any two of the words to make a new sentence.

85

The letters *oi* and *oy* stand for the vowel sound in these words.

coin   **boy**

Write the word that completes each phrase. Circle the letters that stand for the vowel sound.

joy	noise	choice	enjoy	join
point	royal	cowboy	toy	voyage
soil	loyal	oil	voice	annoying

1. a _____ to play with   oi   oy

2. full of happiness and _____   oi   oy

3. need _____ for the squeak   oi   oy

4. to _____ the two ends   oi   oy

5. seeds growing in _____   oi   oy

6. a loud _____   oi   oy

7. the _____ prince and princess   oi   oy

8. her beautiful singing _____   oi   oy

9. a broken pencil _____   oi   oy

10. that _____ rounding up cattle   oi   oy

11. an _____ buzzing sound   oi   oy

12. a _____ between two things   oi   oy

13. a _____ across the ocean   oi   oy

14. to _____ the movie   oi   oy

15. a _____ fan of the football team   oi   oy

Notes for Home: Your child wrote words with the vowel diphthongs *oi* and *oy*.
Home Activity: Take turns with your child using the phrases on the page to make sentences.
Then pick one sentence and use it to begin a story that you make up together.

The letters *oi* and *oy* stand for the vowel sound in *soil* and *boy*.

Write the word from the list that rhymes with the word in the box. Circle the letters that stand for the vowel sound. Then follow the directions.

enjoy   disappoint   royal   coin   voice

1. | join | _____   oi   oy

Add -*ed* to the end of each word.

_____   _____

2. | loyal | _____   oi   oy

Add -*ty* to the end of each word.

_____   _____

3. | employ | _____   oi   oy

Add -*ment* to the end of each word.

_____   _____

4. | anoint | _____   oi   oy

Add -*ing* to the end of each word.

_____   _____

5. | rejoice | _____   oi   oy

Take off the final *e* and add -*ing* to each word.

_____   _____

Notes for Home: Your child wrote words with the vowel diphthongs *oi* and *oy*.
Home Activity: Together list other words that have *oi* or *oy* in them. Take turns with your child naming words that rhyme with the words in the list.

Oil and *joy* have the same vowel sound. The letters *oi* and *oy* stand for that vowel sound.

Write a word from the list next to the word that is almost alike in meaning. Circle the letters that stand for the vowel sound you hear in *oil*.

loyal	toy	toil	oyster
joyful	spoil	join	voyage

1. happy _____   **2.** rot _____

3. faithful _____   **4.** plaything _____

5. connect _____   **6.** work _____

7. shellfish _____   **8.** trip _____

Write a word from the list next to the word that is opposite in meaning. Circle the letters that stand for the vowel sound you hear in *oil*.

destroy	moist	loyal	noisy
boy	unemployed	joy	

9. sadness _____   **10.** girl _____

11. dry _____   **12.** build _____

13. quiet _____   **14.** employed _____

15. disloyal _____

Notes for Home: Your child wrote words with the vowel diphthongs *oi* and *oy*.
Home Activity: Have your child look through newspaper and magazine ads for words with *oi* and *oy*. Read the words together.

A consonant blend with three letters, such as *str, spl,* or *thr,* stands for one sound.

string   **spl**ash   **thr**ee

Use the clues to complete the puzzle.

thread   sprinkler   square   strikes   strawberry
scream   scrub   three   streets   splash

Across

1. used to water a lawn
2. in baseball, three and you are out
5. to wash something by rubbing it hard
6. a red fruit
8. a shape with four equal sides

Down

1. places where cars drive
3. use a needle to sew with this
4. a loud, high yell
5. something people do in a swimming pool
7. the number between two and four

Notes for Home: Your child completed a puzzle, using words with three-letter blends.
Home Activity: Have your child choose one of these blends: *scr, spl, str, squ, spr, thr.*
Together write as many words as you can that begin with the blend.

Name _____

A consonant blend may have three letters that stand for one sound.

scream   **squ**are   **thr**ee

Write each word in the box that has the same three-letter blend.

strong	spring	splash	string	squeak
thrill	throw	stream	squirrel	spray
splinter	square	spread	thread	straw
scratch	split	scream	scrub	three

scr	**spl**
1. _____	4. _____
2. _____	5. _____
3. _____	6. _____

spr	**squ**
7. _____	10. _____
8. _____	11. _____
9. _____	12. _____

str	**thr**
13. _____	17. _____
14. _____	18. _____
15. _____	19. _____
16. _____	20. _____

Notes for Home: Your child sorted words with three-letter blends. **Home Activity:** Take turns with your child choosing any three words from the list at the top of the page and putting the words in alphabetical order.

Name_____

A possessive shows that something belongs to someone or something.

• Add *'s* to make a singular noun possessive.	doctor	doctor**'s**
• Add *'s* to make a plural noun possessive.	men	men**'s**
• Add *'* to a plural noun that ends in *s*.	twins	twins**'**

Make each singular or plural noun possessive.

1. girl _____

2. boy _____

3. Maria _____

4. Lee _____

5. children _____

6. family _____

7. book _____

8. tiger _____

9. herd _____

10. flock _____

Make each plural noun possessive.

11. dogs _____

12. teachers _____

13. shells _____

14. girls _____

15. mice _____

16. geese _____

17. bunnies _____

18. women _____

19. foxes _____

20. cities _____

Notes for Home: Your child wrote possessive forms of singular and plural nouns.
Home Activity: Point to an object. Ask your child to name the object, write its name, say the possessive, and then write it. Example: *book, book's.*

A possessive shows that something belongs to someone or something.

- Add *'s* to make a singular noun possessive.　　cat　　cat's
- Add *'s* to make a plural noun possessive.　　mice　　mice's
- Add *'* to a plural noun that ends in *s*.　　dogs　　dogs'

Change each phrase into a phrase with a possessive.

Example: the stripes of the tiger = the tiger's stripes

1. the tractor that belongs to the farmer　_____

2. a pool for the penguins　_____

3. a pencil that Keesha owns　_____

4. that game that the twins own　_____

5. some seed for the parrots　_____

6. the book belonging to Juan　_____

7. this car belonging to that family　_____

8. a ball that the cat has　_____

9. the flowers belonging to those people　_____

10. the chains for the necklaces　_____

11. a bike for Kwan　_____

12. the park belonging to the community　_____

13. some cages for the lions　_____

14. some shoes belonging to the children　_____

15. this report belonging to the group　_____

Notes for Home: Your child wrote phrases with possessives. **Home Activity:** Take turns with your child writing possessive phrases, such as *Mary's book* or *the dogs' bones.*

Name _____

Here is how to make nouns possessive:

singular noun	sister	sister**'s**
plural noun	women	women**'s**
plural noun ending in *s*	brothers	brothers**'**

Write the possessive noun in each phrase. After each noun, write **S** for singular noun or **P** for plural noun.

1. doctor's office

_____ ___

2. children's games

_____ ___

3. sisters' friend

_____ ___

4. lion's paw

_____ ___

5. men's hats

_____ ___

6. woman's picture

_____ ___

Rewrite each sentence. Use the possessive form of the noun in parentheses.

7. We had a party for my ___ anniversary. (parents)

_____

8. My ___ family came from Tampa. (mother)

_____

9. ___ brother flew in from Dallas. (Dad)

_____

10. Our ___ celebration was a big success. (family)

_____

Notes for Home: Your child identified and wrote possessive nouns.
Home Activity: Have your child look through a favorite book for examples of possessives and tell who owns what.

The letters *oi* and *oy* stand for the vowel sound in *join* and *toy*.

Read each sentence. Write one or two words that have the same vowel sound as *join* and *toy*.

The boys made a lot of noise playing in the yard.

1. _____   2. _____

First, boil the potatoes, and then wrap them in foil.

3. _____   4. _____

Try to join these two coils of rope.

5. _____   6. _____

The cowboy had a loud singing voice.

7. _____   8. _____

The loyal worker was a good employee.

9. _____   10. _____

An oyster tastes good dipped in soy sauce.

11. _____   12. _____

The family enjoyed the sea voyage.

13. _____   14. _____

Use oil to fix the door hinge.

15. _____

Notes for Home: Your child identified and wrote words with *oi* and *oy*.
Home Activity: Have your child choose two words he or she wrote on the page and make up a new sentence using the words.

Name_____

The letters *oi* and *oy* stand for the vowel sound in *join* and *toy*.

Circle 12 hidden words with *oi* and *oy*. Write the words you circle.
Hint: Two words are small words within bigger words.

t	o	y	b	c	m	o	i	s	t	p	o	i	n	t
d	e	f	g	s	p	o	i	l	n	o	i	s	e	h
k	l	b	o	y	m	p	r	s	j	o	y	f	u	l
l	o	y	a	l	s	v	o	i	c	e	g	d	n	s
r	h	v	o	y	a	g	e	b	f	h	m	k	r	s

1. _____   2. _____

3. _____   4. _____

5. _____   6. _____

7. _____   8. _____

9. _____   10. _____

11. _____   12. _____

Write the word from above that means the same as the phrase.

13. a plaything   _____

14. the tip of a pencil   _____

15. very happy   _____

Notes for Home: Your child wrote words with *oi* and *oy*. **Home Activity:** Together make a word-search puzzle like the one on the page. Use words with *oi* and *oy*.

The letters *ar, er, ir, or,* and *ur* stand for the vowel sounds in these words.

ca**rd**   **h**e**r**   **th**i**rd**   **b**or**n**   **t**ur**n**

Write the word that answers each question. Then write the letters that stand for the vowel-*r* sound in the word.

1. Do you eat with a fort or a fork?   _____ _____

2. Would you sir or stir pancake batter?   _____ _____

3. Might you sit on a front port or porch?   _____ _____

4. Does a rabbit have fur or spurs?   _____ _____

5. Could you see a star or a start in the sky?   _____ _____

6. Do you drink water because you are thirsty or thirty? _____ _____

7. Is a gift for or forth someone?   _____ _____

8. Would you turn or burn a candle for light?   _____ _____

9. Do ferns or terms grow in the woods?   _____ _____

10. Does a shirt or a skirt have sleeves?   _____ _____

Notes for Home: Your child wrote vowel-*r* words and identified vowel-*r* spellings.
Home Activity: With your child, look through newspapers. Have your child use a crayon to circle words with *ar, er, ir, or,* and *ur.*

Name_____

The letters *ar, er, ir, or,* and *ur* stand for the vowel sounds in these words.

| st**ar**t | h**er** | f**ir**st | f**or** | t**ur**n |

Write the word from the box that rhymes with each picture name. Then write the letters that stand for the vowel-*r* sound.

| cork | stern | third | fur | dirt |
| jar | thorn | nurse | farm | bark |

1. _____ ___

2. _____ ___

3. _____ ___

4. _____ ___

5. _____ ___

6. _____ ___

7. _____ ___

8.  _____ ___

9. _____ ___

10.  _____ ___

 Notes for Home: Your child wrote *r*-controlled vowel words. **Home Activity:** Take turns with your child drawing pictures of things whose names have *r*-controlled vowel sounds. Help each other write the name for each picture.

Name _____

The letters *ear* and *our* stand for the vowel sounds in these words

learn   **four**

Write each word under the word that has the same vowel-*r* sound. Some words will not be written.

early	pour	court	our	fear
clear	source	heard	course	earth
earn	hour	mourn	search	hear

learn   **four**

1. _____   6. _____

2. _____   7. _____

3. _____   8. _____

4. _____   9. _____

5. _____   10. _____

Write the word from above that completes each phrase.

11. morning and evening; late and _____

12. football and field; basketball and _____

13. locate and seek; find and _____

14. laugh and rejoice; cry and _____

15. looked and saw; listened and _____

Notes for Home: Your child sorted and wrote words with the *r*-controlled vowel patterns *ear* and *our*. **Home Activity:** Use the words in the lists to make up a silly story together.

Name_____

Suffixes are added to the ends of words.

kind**ness**   bright**ly**   help**ful**   humor**ous**

Use a word from the box to complete each tongue twister. Then write the suffix that appears at the end of the word.

sadly	finally	powerful	delightful	poisonous
glamorous	greatness	lively	illness	wonderful

1. Leo Lion likes _____ leaps.   _____

2. Wendy's _____ wagon won.   _____

3. Greta's _____ grew gradually.   _____

4. Firefighters _____ found frisky Fluffy.   _____

5. Sarah sat _____ on the soft, silky sofa.   _____

6. Dora dug _____, dainty daffodils.   _____

7. Inez's _____ is itchy and infectious.   _____

8. Please pull perilous, pesky, _____ plants.   _____

9. Gloria's glimmering, _____ gloves glittered.   _____

10. Pretty, _____ ponies pulled the plows.   _____

Notes for Home: Your child wrote words with suffixes. **Home Activity:** Take turns with your child saying tongue twisters you know. Then make up some tongue twisters that have words with suffixes.

Sometimes when a suffix is added to the end of a word, a spelling change is needed. Sometimes no spelling change is needed.

No spelling change is needed.   kind + ness = kindness
If a word ends in *y*, the *y* is changed to *i*.   beauty – y + i + ful = beautiful

Underline the answer to the question. Write the new word.

1.   **bright**
Does the word end in *y*?   Yes   No
Add **ly.** Write the word.

_____

2.   **happy**
Does the word end in *y*?   Yes   No
Add **ness.** Write the word.

_____

3.   **angry**
Does the word end in *y*?   Yes   No
Add **ly.** Write the word.

_____

4.   **marvel**
Does the word end in *y*?   Yes   No
Add **ous.** Write the word.

_____

5.   **humor**
Does the word end in *y*?   Yes   No
Add **ous.** Write the word.

_____

6.   **fury**
Does the word end in *y*?   Yes   No
Add **ous.** Write the word.

_____

7.   **danger**
Does the word end in *y*?   Yes   No
Add **ous.** Write the word.

_____

8.   **empty**
Does the word end in *y*?   Yes   No
Add **ness.** Write the word.

_____

9.   **easy**
Does the word end in *y*?   Yes   No
Add **ly.** Write the word.

_____

10.   **power**
Does the word end in *y*?   Yes   No
Add **ful.** Write the word.

_____

Notes for Home: Your child added suffixes to words, making spelling changes if necessary. **Home Activity:** Have your child make up a sentence for each word he or she wrote on the page.

Nouns that name more than one person, place, or thing are called plural nouns.

- Add -*s* to most nouns to make them plural.   dog   dog**s**
- Add -*es* to nouns that end in *s, ss, x, ch,* and *sh.*   lunch   lunch**es**

Write the plural of each noun.

1. plane   _____   2. pilot   _____

3. field   _____   4. box   _____

5. wish   _____   6. paper   _____

7. glass   _____   8. shed   _____

9. brush   _____   10. beach   _____

11. week   _____   12. push   _____

13. pass   _____   14. friend   _____

15. circus   _____

Use words you wrote above to complete the sentences.

16. The _____ landed the plane safely.

17. Corn is growing in those _____.

18. How many _____ are in a year?

19. He drank two _____ of milk.

20. How many _____ of cereal are on the shelf?

Notes for Home: Your child formed the plurals of words by adding *s* or *es*.
Home Activity: Take turns with your child pointing to an object, saying the plural form of its name, and writing the plural form.

If a word ends in a vowel and *y, -s* is added to make the word mean more than one.

mon**key** + s = mon**keys**

If a word ends in a consonant and *y,* the *y* is changed to *i,* and *-es* is added to make the word mean more than one.

ba**by** – y + i + es = bab**ies**

Underline *vowel* or *consonant* to answer the question. Then add *-s* or *-es* and write the plural form of the word.

Word	Question	Plural
1. day	Is the letter before *y* a vowel or a consonant?	_____
2. toy	Is the letter before *y* a vowel or a consonant?	_____
3. puppy	Is the letter before *y* a vowel or a consonant?	_____
4. key	Is the letter before *y* a vowel or a consonant?	_____
5. berry	Is the letter before *y* a vowel or a consonant?	_____
6. boy	Is the letter before *y* a vowel or a consonant?	_____
7. bunny	Is the letter before *y* a vowel or a consonant?	_____
8. city	Is the letter before *y* a vowel or a consonant?	_____
9. body	Is the letter before *y* a vowel or a consonant?	_____
10. delay	Is the letter before *y* a vowel or a consonant?	_____

Notes for Home: Your child wrote the plural forms of words ending in *y*.
Home Activity: With your child, look for nouns that end in *y*. Tell how to make the plural. Use the question on the page to help decide whether to make a spelling change.

Some nouns make their plurals in unusual ways.

   1. If the noun ends in *f* or *fe,* the *f* or *fe*
      is changed to *v*, and *-es* is added.   shel**f**   shel**ves**
   2. Some nouns use a new word.   man   men
   3. Some nouns use the same word.   deer   deer

Write **1, 2,** or **3** to tell how each plural was formed. Use the numbered list above.

   1. mouse/mice   _____   **2.** sheep/sheep   _____

   3. wolf/wolves   _____   **4.** woman/women   _____

   5. child/children   _____   **6.** foot/feet   _____

   7. knife/knives   _____   **8.** leaf/leaves   _____

   9. calf/calves   _____   **10.** goose/geese   _____

Write **1, 2,** or **3** to show how to make each word plural. Then write the new word.

   11. wife   _____   _____

   12. tooth   _____   _____

   13. moose   _____   _____

   14. loaf   _____   _____

   15. gentleman   _____   _____

Notes for Home: Your child wrote the plural forms of nouns whose plurals are formed in unusual ways. **Home Activity:** Have your child look in newspapers for plural nouns and tell how each plural was formed. Use the numbered list on the page for help.

Remember how possessive nouns are made:

• For a singular noun, add 's.   aunt   aunt's
• For a plural noun, add 's.   men   men's
• For a plural noun that ends in s, add '.   uncles   uncles'

Write the possessive of the word in parentheses to complete each phrase.

1. (pony)   the _____ mane

2. (schools)   the _____ flags

3. (Smith)   Mrs. _____ house

4. (children)   the _____ books

5. (girls)   the _____ shoes

6. (workers)   the _____ tools

7. (men)   the _____ races

8. (fox)   the _____ tail

9. (sheep)   the _____ wool

10. (women)   the _____ hats

Notes for Home: Your child wrote singular and plural possessive nouns.
Home Activity: Have your child name a person and something he or she might own and then
write the name and the object in a possessive phrase. Example: *Mary book, Mary's book.*

A possessive shows that something belongs to someone or something.

- Add *'s* to make a singular noun possessive.   neighbor   neighbor**'s**
- Add *'s* to make a plural noun possessive.   people   people**'s**
- Add *'* to a plural noun that ends in *s*.   planes   planes**'**

Write the possessive form of each noun. Then add a word to show something that is owned.

Example: swan   swan's   swan's feathers

1. boy   _____   _____

2. cats   _____   _____

3. men   _____   _____

4. mothers   _____   _____

5. bird   _____   _____

6. children   _____   _____

7. turtles   _____   _____

8. teachers   _____   _____

9. chair   _____   _____

10. sister   _____   _____

11. women   _____   _____

12. tree   _____   _____

13. sheep   _____   _____

14. insects   _____   _____

15. mice   _____   _____

Notes for Home: Your child wrote possessive nouns and possessive phrases.
Home Activity: Take turns with your child using the possessive phrases he or she wrote to create oral sentences. Tell which word is the possessive and whether it is singular or plural.

The *k* sound can be spelled by the letters *c*, *ck*, or *ch*.

color ne**ck** **ch**ord

Sort the words to show what letter or letters stand for /k/ in each word.

back	ache	can	stomach	careful
thick	because	cut	vacation	coat
anchor	traffic	echo	track	wreck
bucket	fact	clock	count	recall

/k/ = c

1. _____   2. _____

3. _____   4. _____

5. _____   6. _____

7. _____   8. _____

9. _____   10. _____

/k/ = ck

11. _____   12. _____

13. _____   14. _____

15. _____   16. _____

/k/ = ch

17. _____   18. _____

19. _____   20. _____

Notes for Home: Your child wrote words with /k/ spelled *c, ck,* or *ch.*
Home Activity: With your child, look through the Yellow Pages in a telephone book for words with /k/ spelled *c, ck,* or *ch.*

Name_____

The letters *c, ck,* and *ch* stand for the *k* sound in these words.

           cat   **duck**   **ache**

Write the word in the sentence with /k/. Circle the letter or letters that stand for /k/.

1. Where is my other green sock?   _____

2. My stomach feels full.   _____

3. The chorus sang a happy song.   _____

4. This bucket of water is heavy.   _____

5. My tooth ached all night.   _____

6. Have you ever been camping?   _____

7. Someone left a red jacket on the bus.   _____

8. How high did he count?   _____

9. My friend drives a big truck.   _____

10. What is the name of that chord?   _____

11. The traffic was heavy today.   _____

12. I heard the echo of my voice.   _____

13. My uncle lives in Ohio.   _____

14. What caused the lamp to fall?   _____

15. We need an anchor for the boat.   _____

Notes for Home: Your child identified and wrote words with /k/ spelled *c, ck,* or *ch.*
Home Activity: Have your child choose two /k/ words he or she wrote on the page and use the words in a sentence.

Name_____

The letters _ar, er, ir, or,_ and _ur_ stand for the vowel sounds in these words.

car   **her**   **bird**   **horn**   **turn**

Write the word that belongs in each statement. Then write the letters that stand for the vowel-_r_ sound.

nurse	star	circus	verses	storm
barn	ferns	horse	birthday	fur

1. Farmer: "Every morning I let the cows out of the _____."   _____

2. Doctor: "The _____ will give you your shot."   _____

3. Astronomer: "Light from that _____ takes millions of light-years to reach Earth."   _____

4. Vet: "You need to brush your cat's _____."   _____

5. Gardener: "I find that _____ grow best in shady, moist places."   _____

6. Baker: "Do you want vanilla or chocolate icing on this _____ cake?"   _____

7. Ringmaster: "Welcome to the _____."   _____

8. Jockey: "I knew my _____ could win the race."   _____

9. Poet: "My new poem has seven _____."   _____

10. Weather Forecaster: "We are expecting a major _____ with heavy rain and high winds."   _____

Notes for Home: Your child wrote words with _r_-controlled vowels. **Home Activity:** Help your child make up a new sentence for each word written on the page.

108

Name_____

The letters *air* and *are* stand for the vowel sound in these words.

ch**air**   d**are**

Write the words in the correct order to make sentences. Circle the words with the vowel patterns *air* and *are*.

1. careful Be walking the across street.

_____

2. scared That growling dog me.

_____

3. friends to fair Our the drove us.

_____

4. takes her good She care of goldfish.

_____

5. ice slick the made The stairs.

_____

6. very has ears A long hare.

_____

7. baby silky The blond has hair.

_____

8. a pair got new shoes I of.

_____

9. have a tire spare in Always the car.

_____

10. a flair has for Rosa painting.

_____

Notes for Home: Your child wrote sentences with *air* and *are* words.
Home Activity: Take turns with your child writing a scrambled sentence with an *air* or *are* word and having the other person unscramble the sentence.

The letters *ear* and *our* stand for the vowel sounds in these words.

near   **lear**n   **gour**d

Write the word that goes with the clue. Write the letters that stand for the vowel-*r* sound.

early	hear	mourn	course	fourth
four	source	search	year	court
fear	earth	earn	pour	dear

1. do this with your ears   _____   _____

2. the number after three   _____   _____

3. where something comes from   _____   _____

4. 52 weeks in this   _____   _____

5. the opposite of *late*   _____   _____

6. a path followed   _____   _____

7. to look for   _____   _____

8. a word for *soil*   _____   _____

9. do this with milk   _____   _____

10. a scared feeling   _____   _____

11. feel sad about something   _____   _____

12. to make money   _____   _____

13. a place with judges   _____   _____

14. the place after third   _____   _____

15. word to begin a letter   _____   _____

Notes for Home: Your child wrote words with the vowel patterns *ear* and *our*.
Home Activity: Help your child make a list of words with the vowel sounds and patterns in *near*, *learn*, and *four*. Have your child read the words and name words that rhyme.

When a prefix is added to the beginning of a word, it changes the meaning of the word.

possible	able to be done	**im**possible	**not** able to be done
honest	truthful	**dis**honest	**not** truthful
living	alive	**non**living	**not** alive

Write the word from the box that has the prefix and meaning shown.

> imperfect   disloyal   immovable   nonstop   nonbreakable
> disappear   nonresident   disapprove   impolite   impatient

1. dis + faithful   _____

2. im + able to change its place   _____

3. non + able to be broken   _____

4. im + showing manners   _____

5. dis + come into sight   _____

6. dis + be in favor of   _____

7. non + a person living in a place   _____

8. non + will not halt   _____

9. im + having no mistakes   _____

10. im + willing to wait   _____

Notes for Home: Your child wrote words with the prefixes *im-*, *dis-*, and *non-*.
Home Activity: Have your child name some other words with the prefixes *im-*, *dis-*, and *non-*
and tell what the words mean. Use a dictionary for help.

Name_____

When a prefix is added to the beginning of a word, the spelling of the word does not change.

im + polite = impolite
dis + appear = disappear
non + living = nonliving

Add *im-*, *dis-*, or *non-* to each word to make a new word. Write the new word.

1. possible   _____

2. please   _____

3. agree   _____

4. stop   _____

5. fiction   _____

6. practical   _____

7. honest   _____

8. fat   _____

9. patient   _____

10. proper   _____

Sort the words you wrote above according to their prefixes.

dis-   **non-**

11. _____   14. _____

12. _____   15. _____

13. _____   16. _____

im-

17. _____

18. _____

19. _____

20. _____

Notes for Home: Your child added the prefixes *im-*, *dis-*, and *non-* to words.
Home Activity: Take turns with your child using the words he or she wrote on the page in oral sentences.

Prefixes, such as *im-, dis-,* and *non-*, change the meanings of words.

im + polite	**im**polite	not polite
dis + honest	**dis**honest	not honest
non + breakable	**non**breakable	not breakable

Write the opposite of each word by circling the correct prefix and writing the new word.

	Prefixes			**Word**	**Word with Prefix**
1. im	dis	non		please	_____
2. im	dis	non		possible	_____
3. im	dis	non		stop	_____
4. im	dis	non		like	_____
5. im	dis	non		patient	_____
6. im	dis	non		living	_____
7. im	dis	non		loyal	_____
8. im	dis	non		practical	_____
9. im	dis	non		sense	_____
10. im	dis	non		approve	_____

Notes for Home: Your child added the prefixes *im-, dis-,* and *non-* to words.
Home Activity: Help your child name words that are opposites. Use some words that begin with *im-, dis-,* and *non-*.

Plural nouns can be made in several ways.

- The plurals of most nouns are formed by adding -*s* or -*es*.
- If a noun ends in a vowel and *y*, *s* is added.
- If a noun ends in a consonant and *y*, the *y* is changed to *i*, and -*es* is added.
- The plurals of words ending in *s*, *ss*, *x*, *ch*, or *sh* are formed by adding -*es*.

Write the plural form of the word in parentheses.

1. Our (family) like to have picnics.   _____

2. We all help make the picnic (lunch).   _____

3. My sister likes fruit (salad).   _____

4. I like chicken (sandwich).   _____

5. Dad says we must always bring (cherry).   _____

6. Mom loves cool (glass) of lemonade.   _____

7. We usually have the picnics on (holiday).   _____

8. Each family brings (box) of balls and bats.   _____

9. The boys play on (team) against the girls.   _____

10. These (day) together are wonderful.   _____

Notes for Home: Your child formed the plurals of nouns. **Home Activity:** Together talk about food you both like to eat at picnics. Use plurals as you talk.

Name_____

Some nouns have special plurals.

- The plurals of nouns that end in *f* and *fe* are
  formed by changing *f* or *fe* to *v* and adding *-es*.   shel**f**   shel**ves**
- Sometimes a new word is used for the plural.   man   men
- Sometimes the singular and plural forms are the same.   scissors   scissors

Sort the words to show how each plural was formed.

teeth	women	calves	mice	knives
leaves	sheep	children	wolves	moose
deer	geese	loaves	selves	feet

The *f* or *fe* was changed to *v*. Then *-es* was added.

1. _____   2. _____

3. _____   4. _____

5. _____   6. _____

A new word was used.

7. _____   8. _____

9. _____   10. _____

11. _____   12. _____

The same word is used for singular and plural.

13. _____   14. _____

15. _____

Notes for Home: Your child sorted words to show how plurals were formed.
Home Activity: Work together with your child to add more words to the lists.

When adding the ending *-ed* or *-ing* to words, sometimes a spelling change is needed.

no change	jump	jump**ed**	jump**ing**
drop the final *e*	hop**e**	hop**ed**	hop**ing**
double the final consonant	sto**p**	stop**ped**	stop**ping**
change final *y* to *i*	cr**y**	cr**ied**	
no change	cr**y**	cr**ying**	

Add the ending shown. Write the new word.

Make No Spelling Change

Drop the Final *e*

1. watch (ed) _____

2. lift (ing) _____

3. pack (ed) _____

4. try (ing) _____

5. deny (ing) _____

6. like (ed) _____

7. save (ed) _____

8. smile (ing) _____

9. tire (ed) _____

10. shine (ing) _____

Double the Final Consonant

Change *y* to *i*

11. plan (ed) _____

12. drip (ed) _____

13. run (ing) _____

14. swim (ing) _____

15. get (ing) _____

16. dry (ed) _____

17. worry (ed) _____

18. supply (ed) _____

19. try (ed) _____

20. hurry (ing) _____

Notes for Home: Your child added *-ed* and *-ing* to words. **Home Activity:** Together look through a newspaper or book to find words ending in *-ed* or *-ing*. Have your child tell whether a spelling change was needed when the ending was added to each word.

When the endings *-er* and *-est* are added to words, a spelling change may be needed.

1. no change	great	great**er**	great**est**
2. drop the final *e*	larg**e**	larg**er**	larg**est**
3. double the final consonant	big	big**ger**	big**gest**
4. change final *y* to *i*	happy	happ**ier**	happ**iest**

Write the opposite of each word. Use words from the list. Write **1, 2, 3,** or **4** to show what spelling change, if any, was needed when the ending was added to the answer word.

bigger	easier	hottest	saddest	largest
lightest	driest	youngest	shortest	widest

1. tallest

_____ _____

2. happiest

_____ _____

3. smaller

_____ _____

4. darkest

_____ _____

5. coldest

_____ _____

6. smallest

_____ _____

7. harder

_____ _____

8. oldest

_____ _____

9. narrowest

_____ _____

10. wettest

_____ _____

Notes for Home: Your child wrote words with *-er* and *-est*. **Home Activity:** Name a word ending in *-er* or *-est,* and have your child give its opposite. Then have your child name an *-er* or *-est* word and you give its opposite.

The ending *-er* can be added to words to make them mean "more." The ending *-est* can be added to words to make them mean "most."

deep   deep**er** (more deep)   deep**est** (most deep)

Write the *-er* and *-est* forms of each word. Remember to make these spelling changes if they are needed.

drop the final *e*	large	larg**er**	larg**est**
double the final consonant	big	big**ger**	big**gest**
change final *y* to *i*	happy	happ**ier**	happ**iest**

Word	**More**	**Most**
1. slow	_____	_____
2. funny	_____	_____
3. sad	_____	_____
4. lazy	_____	_____
5. flat	_____	_____
6. brave	_____	_____
7. clean	_____	_____
8. hot	_____	_____
9. easy	_____	_____
10. tame	_____	_____

Notes for Home: Your child wrote words with *-er* and *-est*. **Home Activity:** Work together with your child. Choose a word from the page. Use all three forms in a sentence like this: *I was slow, she was slower, but he was slowest of all.*

The letters *c, ck,* and *ch* spell the *k* sound in these words.

can   du**ck**   a**ch**e

Underline the word in each group that has /k/. In the box, write the letter or letters that stand for /k/ in the word you underlined.

1. cover
   city
   ice

2. chair
   echo
   inch

3. lock
   cheer
   pencil

4. cent
   face
   uncle

5. chord
   chain
   teach

6. peace
   stick
   cheese

7. fact
   center
   dance

8. chase
   anchor
   reach

9. each
   lettuce
   pocket

10. decide
   fancy
   music

Notes for Home: Your child identified words with /k/ spelled *c, ck,* and *ch.*
Home Activity: Take turns with your child giving a meaning clue or a synonym for each underlined word and having the other person name the word.

The letters *c, ck,* and *ch* spell /k/ in *color, dock,* and *ache.*

Write the word that goes with the two words shown. Write the letter or letters that stand for /k/.

cousin	corn	rock	cover	stomach
jacket	complete	truck	cool	bucket
colt	chorus	anchor	duck	trick

1. car, bus

_____ _____

2. mast, deck

_____ _____

3. beans, peas

_____ _____

4. pail, can

_____ _____

5. heart, lungs

_____ _____

6. coat, sweater

_____ _____

7. joke, prank

_____ _____

8. lid, top

_____ _____

9. aunt, uncle

_____ _____

10. calf, lamb

_____ _____

11. cold, chilly

_____ _____

12. singers, choir

_____ _____

13. stone, pebble

_____ _____

14. finish, end

_____ _____

15. goose, swan

_____ _____

Notes for Home: Your child wrote words in which /k/ is spelled *c, ck,* or *ch.*
Home Activity: Take turns with your child naming three things that go together in some way.

Name_____

The letters *wh* stand for the sounds at the beginning of these words.

what   **wh**o

Read each word. Circle *what* if the *wh* in the word sounds like the *wh* in *what*.
Circle *who* if the *wh* in the word sounds like the *wh* in *who*.

1.   **white**   2.   **why**   3.   **whole**

    what   who   what   who   what   who

4.   **wheat**   5.   **whom**   6.   **wheel**

    what   who   what   who   what   who

7.   **whose**   8.   **when**   9.   **where**

    what   who   what   who   what   who

10.   **which**   11.   **whoever**   12.   **while**

    what   who   what   who   what   who

13.   **whirl**   14.   **wholesome**   15.   **whistle**

    what   who   what   who   what   who

Notes for Home: Your child identified words in which *wh* stands for two different sounds.
Home Activity: Together use the words *who, what, when, where,* and *why* to ask each other
questions.

121

The letters *wh* stand for the beginning sound in *wheel*.
The letters *wh* stand for the beginning sound in *whole*.

Write the words in which *wh* stands for the sound in *wheel* around the wheel. Write the words in which *wh* stands for the sound in *whole* on the loaf of whole-wheat bread.

white	who	when	why	whoever
what	where	whirl	whose	whom

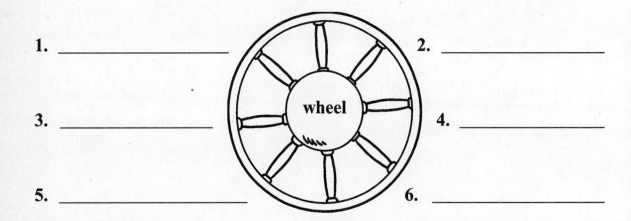

1. _____   2. _____

3. _____   4. _____

5. _____   6. _____

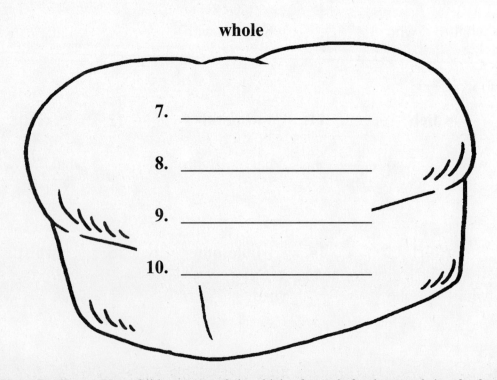

7. _____

8. _____

9. _____

10. _____

Notes for Home: Your child wrote words in which *wh* stands for the sounds in *wheel* and *whole*. **Home Activity:** Take turns with your child scrambling one of the *wh* words from the page and having the other person unscramble the word and write it correctly.

The letters *wh* stand for the beginning sounds in *what* and *who*.

Write the word from the box that rhymes with the numbered word. Then write *what* if the word you wrote has a *wh* that sounds like the *wh* in *what*. Write *who* if the word has a *wh* that sounds like the *wh* in *who*.

1. ten

_____

_____

2. try

_____

_____

3. lose

_____

_____

4. lip

_____

_____

whip
whale
whole
when
where
why
whose
whim
whom
wheat

5. mole

_____

_____

6. sale

_____

_____

7. loom

_____

_____

8. seat

_____

_____

9. pair

_____

_____

10. skim

_____

_____

Notes for Home: Your child wrote words with *wh*. **Home Activity:** Have your child name other rhyming words for the words in the box.

The prefixes *im-, dis-,* and *non-* can be added to the beginnings of words.

im + polite = impolite
dis + appear = disappear
non + living = nonliving

Find and circle a word with the prefix *im-, dis-,* or *non-* in each group of letters.

1. a d r i m p o s s i b l e r s

2. p r e n o n s t o p m e n t s

3. b e a b t e t d i s t r u s t

4. d i s a g r e e a g l e r e d

5. s o r i m p e r f e c t e t o n

Write the words you circled above to complete the sentences.

6. The cracked glass is _____.

7. I _____ with what you said.

8. The acrobat did a trick that looked _____ to do.

9. She is a person I _____.

10. The plane flies _____ to Dallas.

Notes for Home: Your child identified and wrote words with prefixes.
Home Activity: Take turns with your child making up a different sentence for each of the circled words.

The prefixes *im-*, *dis-*, and *non-* change the meaning but not the spelling of a word.

im + polite = impolite   not polite

dis + honest = dishonest   not honest

non + breakable = nonbreakable   not breakable

Add *im-*, *dis-*, or *non-* to make a new word. Then write the meaning of the new word.

1. _____ possible _____

2. _____ loyal _____

3. _____ stop _____

4. _____ patient _____

5. _____ trust _____

6. _____ perfect _____

7. _____ fiction _____

8. _____ pleased _____

9. _____ living _____

10. _____ liked _____

Notes for Home: Your child added prefixes to words and wrote meaning clues for the new words. **Home Activity:** Have your child look in newspapers and magazines for words with the prefixes *im-*, *dis-*, and *non-* and help him or her tell what each word means.

The vowels *a, e, i, o,* and *u* can stand for the vowel sound heard in unaccented syllables. This vowel sound is called the schwa sound. Listen for the schwa sound in these words.

about   tak**e**n   penc**i**l   mel**o**n   circ**u**s

Write the vowel that stands for the schwa sound in each word.

1. ago _____   **2.** kitchen _____   **3.** today _____

4. focus _____   **5.** cabin _____   **6.** number _____

7. major _____   **8.** allow _____   **9.** useful _____

10. dollar _____   **11.** fallen _____   **12.** actor _____

Match the beginning of each sentence to its ending. Write each sentence. Circle two words with the schwa sound.

I got two gallons of milk   as citrus fruit.

Lemons are known   tuna salad sandwich.

I made one tasty   at Al's grocery store.

13. _____

14. _____

15. _____

Notes for Home: Your child identified words with the schwa sound.
Home Activity: Have your child tell you how he or she thinks a favorite dish is prepared. Listen for and call attention to words used that have the schwa sound.

Name_____

The vowels *a, e, i, o,* and *u* can stand for the schwa sound. Listen for the schwa sound in these words.

about   taken   pencil   lemon   circus

Write the words in each box that have the schwa sound.

Animals

zebra   1. _____

horse   2. _____

otter   3. _____

parakeet

Clothes

shirt   4. _____

trousers   5. _____

sweater   6. _____

slippers

Number Words

seven   7. _____

thirty   8. _____

eleven   9. _____

hundred

Buildings

skyscraper   10. _____

cabin   11. _____

apartment   12. _____

house

Food

apple   13. _____

banana   14. _____

bread   15. _____

chicken

Notes for Home: Your child identified words with the schwa sound.
Home Activity: With your child, name other words that could be included in each category. Check to see if any of them have the schwa sound.

The letters *a, e, i, o,* and *u* stand for the schwa sound in these words.

about   tak**e**n   rob**i**n   lem**o**n   circ**u**s

Write the word for each picture. Then write the letter that stands for the schwa sound.

sweater	apple	pencil	carrot	cactus
cabin	seven	zebra	walrus	wagon

1.

_____

2.

_____

3.

_____

4.

_____

5.

_____

6.

_____

7.

_____

8.

_____

9.

_____

10.

_____

Notes for Home: Your child wrote words and the letters that stand for the schwa sound.
Home Activity: With your child, look in a magazine for pictures of things whose names have the schwa sound.

The letters *wh* stand for the beginning sounds in these words.

what   **wh**o

Put a check by each word in which *wh* stands for the same sound as in the word at the top of the box.

what		who	
1. white	_____	11. whom	_____
2. whale	_____	12. while	_____
3. wheel	_____	13. wharf	_____
4. when	_____	14. whoever	_____
5. whole	_____	15. which	_____
6. where	_____	16. wholesome	_____
7. whether	_____	17. why	_____
8. whose	_____	18. wholly	_____
9. whistle	_____	19. whip	_____
10. whirl	_____	20. wholesale	_____

Write a word you checked above to complete each sentence.

21. The kitten is black with _____ paws.

22. Wheat bread is often thought to be a _____ food.

23. To _____ is this gift to be sent?

24. The referee blew a _____ because of a foul.

25. A _____ is a large sea mammal.

The letters *wh* stand for two different sounds: the sound heard in *what* and the sound heard in *who*.

Circle the *wh* word or words in each question. Then answer the question. If you are not sure, make up your own answer.

1. Where did Little Miss Muffet sit?

_____

2. Who did Simple Simon meet?

_____

3. Whose mittens were lost?

_____

4. What followed Mary to school?

_____

5. Why did Jack and Jill go up a hill?

_____

6. Where was the cow while Little Boy Blue was asleep?

_____

7. By when was the cobbler to have the shoe mended?

_____

8. For whom did Old Mother Hubbard go to the cupboard?

_____

9. Which animal—the cow or the cat—jumped over the moon?

_____

10. Who wanted to see whether they could put Humpty Dumpty together again?

_____

Notes for Home: Your child wrote words with *wh*. **Home Activity:** Say some nursery rhymes with your child such as "Mary Had a Little Lamb" or "Little Miss Muffet." Point out any *wh* words you say.

Name_____

To count the number of syllables in a word, count the number of vowel sounds you hear.

side	one vowel sound	=	one syllable
teacher	two vowel sounds	=	two syllables
uniform	three vowel sounds	=	three syllables

Look at and say the picture name. Write the number of vowels you **see** in the first box. Write the number of vowels you **hear** in the second box. Write the number of syllables in the word in the third box.

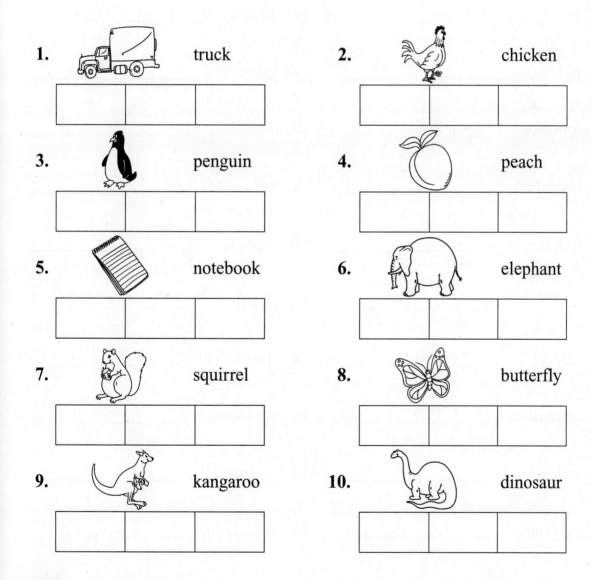

1. truck

2. chicken

3. penguin

4. peach

5. notebook

6. elephant

7. squirrel

8. butterfly

9. kangaroo

10. dinosaur

Notes for Home: Your child counted the number of syllables in words.
Home Activity: Take turns with your child naming an object in the room and telling how many syllables are in its name.

Sometimes dividing a word into parts can help you read a word you do not know.

- Divide between the two smaller words in a compound word.

  doghouse   dog/house

- Divide between a prefix, a suffix, or an ending and the base word.

  re/read   pay/ment   un/fold/ed   care/less/ness

Rewrite the words. Use slashes to show where to divide the words.

1. graceful _____

2. birthday _____

3. popcorn _____

4. softly _____

5. unlucky _____

6. inside _____

7. breakfast _____

8. weekend _____

9. maybe _____

10. unpack _____

11. bedroom _____

12. unsafe _____

13. airport _____

14. cheerful _____

15. distrustful _____

16. unkindness _____

17. unsafely _____

18. backyard _____

19. playfully _____

20. moonlight _____

Notes for Home: Your child divided compound words and words with affixes into syllables.
Home Activity: Help your child list some compound words and divide each word into
syllables by drawing slashes between syllables.

Name_____

Sometimes looking for small parts in a big word can help you read the word.

- Look for affixes.   **un**/like/**ly**   **re**/place/**ment**
- Look for little words you already know.   **out**/ward   **ten**/sion
- Look for familiar vowel patterns.   mon/s**oo**n   pro/c**ee**d   re/b**ate**

Write the syllables of each word on the lines below. One syllable is already written for you.

independent	emergency	embarrassment
receptionist	spitefulness	reconstruction
neighborhood	convenience	establishment
photosynthesis	electromagnet	gymnastics
splendidly	prescription	unhappiness

1. _____ / _____ / ly

2. es / _____ / _____ / _____

3. _____ / _____ / _____ / the / _____

4. _____ / _____ / tics

5. _____ / _____ / pi / _____

6. _____ / _____ / _____ / ist

7. _____ / _____ / tro / _____ / _____

8. em / _____ / _____ / _____

9. _____ / _____ / struc / _____

10. _____ / ful / _____

11. _____ / _____ / i / _____

12. _____ / de / _____ / _____

13. _____ / scrip / _____

14. _____ / _____ / _____ / cy

15. _____ / bor / _____

Notes for Home: Your child divided words into syllables. **Home Activity:** Have your child look through a newspaper article and highlight words with three or more syllables.

When adding the ending *-ed* or *-ing*, the spelling of a word sometimes has to be changed.

start, start**ed**, start**ing**	no change
hope, hop**ed**, hop**ing**	drop the final *e*
stop, stop**ped**, stop**ping**	double the final consonant
try, tr**ied**	change *y* to *i*
try, try**ing**	no change

Add *-ed* or *-ing* to each word in the box to make a word that completes each sentence. Write the new word.

swim	fly	hurry	chase	laugh
hop	paint	move	cry	study

1. She _____ hard for the spelling test.

2. Let's go _____ in the pool to cool off.

3. Who _____ into the house next to yours?

4. The unhappy baby started _____ again.

5. In the movie, a kangaroo was _____ over a fence.

6. Our dog _____ the squirrel up the tree.

7. I like _____ pictures of dinosaurs with my watercolor set.

8. We saw some geese _____ south.

9. I _____ outside, so I would not miss the bus.

10. We were all _____ at the silly joke.

Notes for Home: Your child added the endings *-ed* and *-ing* to words, making spelling changes where needed. **Home Activity:** Take turns with your child telling about something you like to do. See how many *-ed* and *-ing* words you use.

Name _____

Adding *-er* to some words can make them mean "more."
Add *-est* to some words can make them mean "most."

sad   sadd**er** (more sad)   sadd**est** (most sad)

Add *-er* or *-est* to make each word mean "more" or "most." Remember to make
spelling changes if necessary.

1. most big

_____

2. more wide

_____

3. most dry

_____

4. more light

_____

5. most tall

_____

6. most large

_____

7. more heavy

_____

8. more old

_____

9. more tame

_____

10. more quick

_____

11. most flat

_____

12. most wet

_____

13. more brave

_____

14. most easy

_____

15. more muddy

_____

Notes for Home: Your child wrote words ending in *-er* and *-est*. **Home Activity:** Have your
child list ten words that end with *-er* and ten words that end with *-est* and then use "more" and
"most" to tell what each word means.

The letters *aw, au,* and *al* stand for the vowel sound in these words.

dr*aw* **c*au*se** **h*all***

Write the letters that stand for the vowel sound you hear in *draw* in each word. Underline *beginning, middle,* or *end* to show where you hear that vowel sound.

1. raw _____

beginning   middle   end

2. talk _____

beginning   middle   end

3. small _____

beginning   middle   end

4. awesome _____

beginning   middle   end

5. lawn _____

beginning   middle   end

6. thaw _____

beginning   middle   end

7. paw _____

beginning   middle   end

8. salt _____

beginning   middle   end

9. stall _____

beginning   middle   end

10. falling _____

beginning   middle   end

11. sauce _____

beginning   middle   end

12. pause _____

beginning   middle   end

13. claws _____

beginning   middle   end

14. walk _____

beginning   middle   end

15. because _____

beginning   middle   end

Notes for Home: In this activity, your child identified the *aw, au,* and *al* vowel patterns in words. **Home Activity:** Take turns with your child naming a word on the page and then naming another word on the page with the same vowel sound and spelling.

Name _____

The same vowel sound can be spelled by different letter pairs.

draw   **cau**se   **hall**

Add the letters *aw, au,* or *al* to make the words in the list.

baseball	draw	author	auto	false
hawk	fall	chalk	straw	faucet

1. h ___ ___ k

2. dr ___ ___

3. f ___ ___ l

4. ___ ___ to

5. ch ___ ___ k

6. str ___ ___

7. baseb ___ ___ l

8. ___ ___ thor

9. f ___ ___ se

10. f ___ ___ cet

Write the word from above that goes with each clue.

11. Use this to write on the board.   _____

12. A pitcher throws this.   _____

13. This is a kind of bird.   _____

14. This is another word for *car.*   _____

15. Turn on water with this.   _____

16. To make a picture, do this.   _____

17. It is the opposite of *true.*   _____

18. You can drink through this.   _____

19. If you trip, you might do this.   _____

20. This person writes books.   _____

Notes for Home: Your child identified and wrote words with the *aw, au,* and *al* vowel patterns. **Home Activity:** Both you and your child should draw a picture for one of the words on the page. Together tell a story to go with each picture.

137

Draw, cause, and *hall* all have the same vowel sound. But different letters stand for the vowel sound in each word.

Write the word that belongs in each group. Then write the letters that stand for the vowel sound you hear in *draw*.

auto	pause	August	chalk	autumn
baseball	walnut	small	draw	also
hawk	author	straw	auditorium	gnaw

1. little, tiny, _____ _____

2. bus, truck, _____ _____

3. paint, color, _____ _____

4. football, basketball, _____ _____

5. wait, rest, _____ _____

6. board, eraser, _____ _____

7. arena, theater, _____ _____

8. eagle, falcon, _____ _____

9. bite, chew, _____ _____

10. acorn, cashew, _____ _____

11. spring, summer, _____ _____

12. in addition, too, _____ _____

13. writer, poet, _____ _____

14. June, July, _____ _____

15. grass, hay, _____ _____

Notes for Home: Your child wrote words with the *aw, au,* and *al* vowel patterns.
Home Activity: Help your child make up other groups of three words and tell how the words go together.

The vowels—*a, e, i, o, u*—can stand for a vowel sound called the schwa sound. You hear the schwa sound in unaccented syllables. Listen for the schwa sound in these words.

zebr**a**   sweat**e**r   penc**i**l   lem**o**n   circ**u**s

Write each word under the word that has the same spelling for the schwa sound.

grocery	tuna	eleven	carrot	citrus
awful	tractor	cabin	salad	focus
cabinet	vessel	stencil	allow	actor

        zebr**a**      sweat**e**r

1. _____   4. _____

2. _____   5. _____

3. _____   6. _____

        penc**i**l   lem**o**n

7. _____   10. _____

8. _____   11. _____

9. _____   12. _____

        circ**u**s

13. _____

14. _____

15. _____

 Notes for Home: Your child sorted words according to the spelling of their schwa sound. **Home Activity:** Help your child use a dictionary to find ten more words with the schwa sound. (The schwa symbol is /ə/ in a dictionary.)

The vowels *a, e, i, o,* and *u* stand for the schwa sound in these words.

about   tak**e**n   penc**i**l   lem**o**n   circ**u**s

Complete each rhyme by writing a word from the list with the schwa sound. Circle the letter that stands for the schwa sound.

tractor   liver   ago   wagon   awful
cabinet   eleven   bacon   liner   slippers

1. Lots of white, fluffy snow

Fell not too long _____.   a   e   i   o   u

2. There are tiny silver zippers

On the fancy bedroom _____.   a   e   i   o   u

3. I ate only a tiny sliver

Of the big piece of _____.   a   e   i   o   u

4. Dad used the Internet

To buy a wooden _____.   a   e   i   o   u

5. In the movie the actor

Had to drive a big green _____.   a   e   i   o   u

6. She just turned seven,

But I am not _____.   a   e   i   o   u

7. There is nothing finer

Than a trip on an ocean _____.   a   e   i   o   u

8. The gentle striped dragon

Was pulling a _____.   a   e   i   o   u

9. So much gum all in one jawful

Gave me a pain that was _____.   a   e   i   o   u

10. If I am not mistaken,

That wonderful smell is _____.   a   e   i   o   u

Notes for Home: Your child wrote words with the schwa sound to complete rhymes.
Home Activity: Take turns with your child choosing another word with the schwa sound and making up a rhyme for the word.

The letters *ui* and *ew* stand for the vowel sound in these words

br**ui**se   bl**ew**

Write the word from the box that means the same as the clue. Then circle the letters *ui* or *ew* that stand for the vowel sound.

newspaper	suit	crew	new	drew
juice	grew	cruise	fruit	chew

1. sail from place to place   _____

2. what someone did who is now taller   _____

3. apples, bananas, and grapes, for example   _____

4. never used   _____

5. liquid from an orange or other fruit   _____

6. jacket and pants that go together   _____

7. something to read that has today's information _____

8. people who work together as a team   _____

9. what someone did who sketched a picture   _____

10. what the dog did to a bone   _____

Notes for Home: Your child wrote words with the vowel patterns *ui* and *ew*.
Home Activity: Have your child choose some words from the box and use them to begin a story. Then take turns adding to the story.

In *suit,* the vowel sound is spelled *ui.* In *new,* the same vowel sound is spelled *ew.*

Follow the directions to make new words. Then circle the letters that stand for the vowel sound.

1. Start with **bruise.**
   Take away the **b.**
   Add **c.** Write the new word.

   _____

2. Start with **crew.**
   Take away the **cr.**
   Add **dr.** Write the new word.

   _____

3. Start with **fruit.**
   Take away the **fr.**
   Add **s.** Write the new word.

   _____

4. Start with **blew.**
   Take away the **bl.**
   Add **ch.** Write the new word.

   _____

5. Start with **flew.**
   Take away the **fl.**
   Add **gr.** Write the new word.

   _____

6. Start with **judo.**
   Take away the **do.**
   Add **ice.** Write the new word.

   _____

7. Start with **grew.**
   Take away the **gr.**
   Add **bl.** Write the new word.

   _____

8. Start with **drew.**
   Take away the **d.**
   Add **c.** Write the new word.

   _____

9. Start with **suit.**
   Take away the **s.**
   Add **fr.** Write the new word.

   _____

10. Start with **cruise.**
    Take away the **cr.**
    Add **br.** Write the new word.

    _____

Notes for Home: Your child wrote words with the vowel patterns *ui* and *ew.*
Home Activity: Have your child use two of the *ui* or *ew* words from the page to write a rhyme.

142

The letters *ui* and *ew* stand for the vowel sound in *bruise* and *chew*.

Write the word from the box that completes each phrase. Circle the letters that stand for a vowel sound.

juice	drew	suit	grew	flew
new	fruit	crew	cruise	blew

1. rode my brand-_____ bike ui ew

2. _____ a picture of our cat ui ew

3. drank some fresh orange _____ ui ew

4. ate a banana from a bowl of _____ ui ew

5. the _____ of the space shuttle ui ew

6. geese that _____ over our house ui ew

7. jacket for a business _____ ui ew

8. winds that _____ 40 miles per hour ui ew

9. _____ vegetables to eat ui ew

10. take a _____ to Bermuda ui ew

Notes for Home: Your child wrote words with the *ui* and *ew* vowel patterns.
Home Activity: Take turns with your child making up new phrases or sentences for each word in the box.

Dividing words into syllables may help you read words you do not know.

- To count the number of syllables in a word, count the number of vowel sounds.
- Divide between the two smaller words in a compound word.

  doghouse   dog/house
- Divide between a prefix, a suffix, or an ending and the base word.

  re/read   go/ing   dis/place/ment   care/less/ness

Write each word under the heading that tells how many syllables it has. Then draw
lines to show how to divide each word into syllables.

repayment	distrustful	unkindness	outside	unsafely
crying	unfairness	homework	leadership	playground
sunglasses	displeased	careless	replace	rebuilding
doing	crewmate	mistreatment	playfully	meanwhile

Two-Syllable Words

1. _____   2. _____

3. _____   4. _____

5. _____   6. _____

7. _____   8. _____

9. _____   10. _____

Three-Syllable Words

11. _____   12. _____

13. _____   14. _____

15. _____   16. _____

17. _____   18. _____

19. _____   20. _____

Notes for Home: Your child sorted two- and three-syllable words and divided the words into
syllables. **Home Activity:** Have your child find some two- and three-syllable words in a
newspaper or magazine.

Name_____

Sometimes looking for small parts in a big word can help you read the word.

- Look for affixes.   **un**/like/**ly**   **re**/place/**ment**
- Look for little words you already know.   **out**/ward   **ten**/sion
- Look for familiar vowel patterns.   mon/**soo**n   pro/**cee**d   re/**ba**te

Match each word with a clue. Write the word in syllables.

unhealthy	subtraction	Tennessee	illustrate	imprison
skeleton	televise	reminder	basketball	endlessly
chimpanzee	yesterday	promotion	Washington	pantomime

1. a southern state   _____ / _____ / _____

2. never stopping   _____ / _____ / _____

3. 25 − 11 = 13   _____ / _____ / _____

4. gestures without words   _____ / _____ / _____

5. broadcast on TV   _____ / _____ / _____

6. movement to a higher level   _____ / _____ / _____

7. small ape   _____ / _____ / _____

8. game played with a large, round ball   _____ / _____ / _____

9. all the bones in the body   _____ / _____ / _____

10. not well   _____ / _____ / _____

11. make pictures for   _____ / _____ / _____

12. the day before today   _____ / _____ / _____

13. put in prison   _____ / _____ / _____

14. something to help you remember   _____ / _____ / _____

15. first U.S. president   _____ / _____ / _____

Notes for Home: Your child divided words into syllables. **Home Activity:** Take turns with your child finding a long word in a story and dividing it into syllables. Be sure to check your answers in a dictionary.

When an affix is added to a word, a spelling change may or may not be needed.

- **Prefixes**
  no spelling change   happy   **un**happy
- **Suffixes and Endings**
  no spelling change   go   go**ing**
  drop the final *e*   hope   hop**ing**
  double the final consonant   big   big**ger**
  change *y* to *i*   happy   happ**iness**

Add the affix or affixes shown. Write the new word.

1. The dinner tasted (wonder + ful).   _____

2. I could hardly wait to (un + wrap) the gift.   _____

3. She sang (happy + ly) all morning.   _____

4. The kitchen faucet is (drip + ing).   _____

5. The (smile + ing) baby laughed.   _____

6. I (like + ed) the movie.   _____

7. Where is the (swim + ing) pool?   _____

8. The sun was shining (bright + ly).   _____

9. They were (dis + please + ed) with the work.   _____

10. She slept (un + easy + ly) through the storm.   _____

Notes for Home: Your child added affixes—prefixes, suffixes, and endings—to words.
Home Activity: Together with your child choose one of the sentences and use it to begin a story. Try to use words with affixes as you tell the story.

Name_____

A word may have one or more affixes added to it.

Prefix	**Suffix**	**Ending**	**More Than One Affix**
disappear	appear**ance**	appear**ing**	**dis**appear**ance**

Write each word to show what affixes were added.

sickness   unhappy   incorrectly   unpacking   repainted
drawing   shortest   distrusted   impolitely   sadly

Prefix	**Base Word**	**Suffix or Ending**
1. _____	_____	_____
2. _____	_____	_____
3. _____	_____	_____
4. _____	_____	_____
5. _____	_____	_____
6. _____	_____	_____
7. _____	_____	_____
8. _____	_____	_____
9. _____	_____	_____
10. _____	_____	_____

Notes for Home: Your child identified affixes—prefixes, suffixes, and endings—in words. **Home Activity:** Together with your child look through a favorite book for words with affixes. Take turns naming the base word and the affixes added.

Name _____

When affixes are added to words, a spelling change may be needed.

Underline the word in the sentence that has an affix or affixes added. Then write the base word and the affixes.

1. I disagree with your idea.

   Base Word _____ Affix or Affixes _____

2. That is the biggest snake I have ever seen.

   Base Word _____ Affix or Affixes _____

3. They cried when they heard the sad story.

   Base Word _____ Affix or Affixes _____

4. I like a movie that is humorous.

   Base Word _____ Affix or Affixes _____

5. She is hoping to go to the park.

   Base Word _____ Affix or Affixes _____

6. Our team was victorious.

   Base Word _____ Affix or Affixes _____

7. Who uncovered the treasure chest?

   Base Word _____ Affix or Affixes _____

8. Why are you displeased with the book?

   Base Word _____ Affix or Affixes _____

9. The huge rock is immovable.

   Base Word _____ Affix or Affixes _____

10. We sat impatiently because the play did not begin on time.

   Base Word _____ Affix or Affixes _____

Notes for Home: Your child identified base words and affixes—prefixes, suffixes, and endings. **Home Activity:** Together with your child look through junk mail for examples of words with affixes. Tell what the base word is and what affixes were added.

Name_____

The letters *aw, au,* and *al* stand for the vowel sound in these words.

| dr**aw** | c**au**se | h**al**l |

Draw lines to match two rhyming words with the same spelling for the vowel sound.

1. call	talk	**6.** claw	dawn
2. walk	law	**7.** salt	halt
3. lawn	wall	**8.** haul	waltz
4. cause	drawn	**9.** false	flaw
5. paw	pause	**10.** yawn	Paul

Write each pair of words you matched above. Write the letters that stand for the vowel sound.

Words   **Vowel Sound**

11. _____ and _____ _____

12. _____ and _____ _____

13. _____ and _____ _____

14. _____ and _____ _____

15. _____ and _____ _____

16. _____ and _____ _____

17. _____ and _____ _____

18. _____ and _____ _____

19. _____ and _____ _____

20. _____ and _____ _____

Notes for Home: Your child matched rhyming words with *aw, au,* and *al.*
Home Activity: Together with your child use pairs of words from the page to make up silly rhymes.

149

Name_____

The letters *aw, au,* and *al* stand for the vowel sound in *draw, cause,* and *hall.*

Write the word that answers the question. Circle the letters that stand for the vowel sound you hear in *draw.*

1. Can chalk or yawns squeak? _____

2. Does a snake crawl or walk? _____

3. Could a person drive a straw or an auto? _____

4. Does the lawn or the hall get mowed? _____

5. Would you call or draw a picture? _____

6. Can an author or an altar write a book? _____

7. Is a skyscraper tall or small? _____

8. Would you eat a scrawl or a walnut? _____

9. Is a horse kept in a crawl or a stall? _____

10. Would you cook sauce or chalk? _____

11. Do claws or hawks fly? _____

12. Would you hit a flaw or a baseball? _____

13. Do you wash laundry or lawyers? _____

14. Would you turn on a faucet or a pause? _____

15. Would you sit in an auditorium or a drawer? _____

Notes for Home: Your child wrote words with the vowel patterns *aw, au,* and *al.*
Home Activity: Take turns with your child choosing a word that was not an answer on the page and asking a question about the word.

Panel 1 (top-left)

The letter *a* stands for the short *a* vowel sound in *cat*.
The letter *e* stands for the short *e* vowel sound in *net*.
The letter *i* stands for the short *i* vowel sound in *hit*.

Say each picture name. Write the letter that stands for the vowel sound.

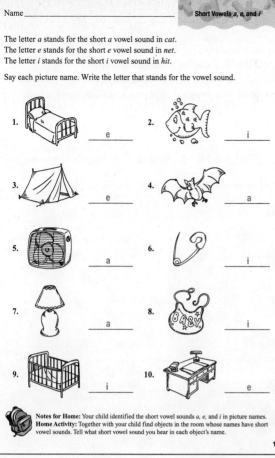

1. ___e___   2. ___i___

3. ___e___   4. ___a___

5. ___a___   6. ___i___

7. ___a___   8. ___i___

9. ___i___   10. ___e___

Notes for Home: Your child identified the short vowel sounds *a, e,* and *i* in picture names.
Home Activity: Together with your child find objects in the room whose names have short vowel sounds. Tell what short vowel sound you hear in each object's name.

1

Panel 2 (top-right)

The letter *o* stands for the short *o* vowel sound in *hot*.
The letter *u* stands for the short *u* vowel sound in *luck*.

Underline the words with the same vowel sound as the first word in the row. Then follow the directions.

hot 1. <u>clock</u>   rose   roll   <u>rock</u>

2. Write two words that rhyme with *hot*.   Answers for rhyming words will vary.
   not   pot

run 3. <u>sum</u>   cute   turn   <u>must</u>

4. Write two words that rhyme with *run*.
   fun   sun

mug 5. count   <u>cut</u>   <u>cup</u>   cube

6. Write two words that rhyme with *mug*.
   rug   bug

not 7. hold   <u>knob</u>   load   <u>stop</u>

8. Write two words that rhyme with *not*.
   hot   cot

lock 9. <u>top</u>   <u>pond</u>   bowl   stove

10. Write two words that rhyme with *lock*.
    clock   rock

Notes for Home: Your child identified words with the short vowel sounds *o* and *u*.
Home Activity: Have your child make up sentences using the words in dark type.

2

Panel 3 (bottom-left)

The letters *a, e, i, o,* and *u* stand for the short vowel sounds in words.

cat   net   hit   hot   luck

Underline two words that have the same short vowel sound as the word at the beginning of the row.

1. trick   lion   <u>quit</u>   shirt   <u>gift</u>

2. spent   <u>next</u>   <u>center</u>   deep   knee

3. stamp   game   salt   <u>stand</u>   <u>after</u>

4. rock   <u>job</u>   home   note   <u>stop</u>

5. just   fur   music   <u>summer</u>   <u>sudden</u>

6. fast   table   <u>band</u>   <u>ask</u>   wait

7. left   each   sleep   <u>empty</u>   <u>set</u>

8. fun   <u>number</u>   excuse   <u>study</u>   fuel

9. cot   coin   enjoy   <u>clock</u>   <u>cannot</u>

10. inch   bike   <u>this</u>   <u>until</u>   time

Notes for Home: Your child identified words with short vowel sounds. **Home Activity:** Have your child choose a favorite book and name words from that book that have short vowel sounds.

3

Panel 4 (bottom-right)

Sometimes the spelling of a base word changes when *-ed* is added.

jump—jumped no change
clap—clapped double the final consonant

chase—chased drop the final *e*
try—tried change *y* to *i*

Write each *-ed* word under the heading that tells what happened to the base word when *-ed* was added.

slipped   relaxed   captured   worried   shared
carried   stopped   played   discovered   studied

No Change

1. relaxed
2. played
3. discovered

Dropped the Final *e*

4. captured
5. shared

Doubled the Final Consonant

6. slipped
7. stopped

Changed *y* to *i*

8. carried
9. worried
10. studied

Notes for Home: Your child added the *-ed* ending to words. **Home Activity:** Have your child write words that end in *-ed*. Talk about what spelling changes, if any, were needed before the *-ed* ending was added.

4

Answers **151**

Sometimes the spelling of a base word changes when -*ing* is added.

jump—jump**ing**   no change
smile—smil**ing**   drop the final *e*
hop—hop**ping**   double the final consonant

Add -*ing* to each word. Write the new word on the line.

1. charge ___charging___   2. win ___winning___

3. recite ___reciting___   4. discover ___discovering___

5. get ___getting___   6. circle ___circling___

7. visit ___visiting___   8. strum ___strumming___

9. ride ___riding___   10. sing ___singing___

Write the word from above that completes each sentence.

11. On my summer vacation, I will be ___visiting___ a ranch.

12. I will be ___getting___ a new pair of cowboy boots for the trip.

13. Each day I will go ___riding___ on a horse.

14. Maybe I will even try ___strumming___ a guitar.

15. I will be ___discovering___ many new things.

Notes for Home: Your child added the -*ing* ending to words. **Home Activity:** Take turns with your child telling a story about a family trip you would like to take. Use words ending in -*ing*.

5

Some words have double consonants in the middle: *butter, dinner*. The two consonants stand for one sound.

Underline the words with double consonants in the middle.

1. little	2. follow	3. pepper	4. double	5. different
6. sorry	7. three	8. batter	9. tomorrow	10. kitchen
11. pretty	12. forest	13. wheel	14. happy	15. summer

Write the opposite of each word. Use a word from the box.

16. same ___different___   17. salt ___pepper___

18. pitcher ___batter___   19. lead ___follow___

20. glad ___sorry___   21. ugly ___pretty___

22. big ___little___   23. sad ___happy___

24. today ___tomorrow___   25. winter ___summer___

Notes for Home: Your child identified words with double consonants in the middle. **Home Activity:** Have your child choose a word he or she wrote and give another word that has a similar meaning.

6

Some words have double consonants at the end: *still, gruff*. The two consonants stand for one sound.

Write the two letters that stand for the ending sound in each picture name.

1. ___ss___   2. ___ll___

3. ___gg___   4. ___ss___

5. ___ll___   6. ___tt___

7. ___ff___   8. ___ll___

9. ___ll___   10. ___ss___

Notes for Home: Your child identified words with double consonants at the end. **Home Activity:** Have your child look through a magazine and find other words that have double consonants at the end.

7

The *a*-consonant-*e* pattern stands for the long *a* vowel sound.

bake   same

Underline each word with the long *a* sound spelled *a*-consonant-*e*. Then use the underlined words to complete the story.

1. made   2. day   3. fame   4. safe

5. way   6. name   7. paid   8. take

9. came   10. trail   11. pale   12. ate

13. Goldilocks is a girl's ___name___.

14. She gained ___fame___ in a story about three bears.

15. One day she ___came___ to a house in the woods.

16. She ___ate___ some of the bears' porridge.

17. Goldilocks ___made___ herself comfortable by sitting in their chairs.

18. Then she tried to ___take___ a nap.

19. When she saw the bears, she turned ___pale___.

20. She ran from the house until she was ___safe___.

Notes for Home: Your child wrote words with the long *a* vowel sound spelled *a*-consonant-*e*. **Home Activity:** Take turns with your child telling a favorite story. Listen for words with the long *a* sound and name them.

8

---

152 Answers

Name_____

The *i*-consonant-*e* pattern stands for the long *i* vowel sound.

nice   fine

Draw a line from each picture to the word for the picture.

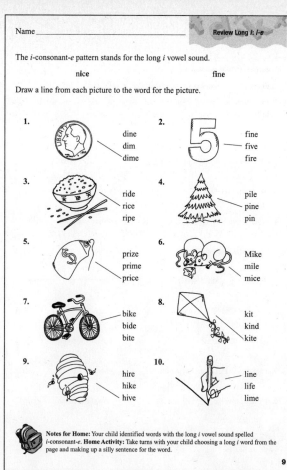

1. dine
    dim
    dime

2. fine
    five
    fire

3. ride
    rice
    ripe

4. pile
    pine
    pin

5. prize
    prime
    price

6. Mike
    mile
    mice

7. bike
    bide
    bite

8. kit
    kind
    kite

9. hire
    hike
    hive

10. line
    life
    lime

Notes for Home: Your child identified words with the long *i* vowel sound spelled *i*-consonant-*e*. **Home Activity:** Take turns with your child choosing a long *i* word from the page and making up a silly sentence for the word.

9

Name_____

The *o*-consonant-*e* pattern stands for the long *o* vowel sound.

woke   hope

Write the word that answers each clue and has the long *o* sound spelled *o*-consonant-*e*.

1. something to wear to keep warm
    robe   coat   robe

2. a place to live
    house   home   home

3. a holder for ice cream
    cone   carton   cone

4. something a cowhand uses
    rope   road   rope

5. a beautiful flower
    rose   daffodil   rose

6. a place to cook
    stove   pot   stove

7. something you might break if you fall
    bone   toe   bone

8. where electric wires might be hung
    post   pole   pole

9. a part of your face
    eyebrows   nose   nose

10. a way to look at the stars
    window   telescope   telescope

Notes for Home: Your child wrote words with the long *o* vowel sound spelled *o*-consonant-*e*. **Home Activity:** With your child, make up meaning clues for these long *o* words: *stone, vote, globe, hose.*

10

Name_____

The long *e* sound can be spelled *ee, ea, ie,* and *ey.*

teeth   teach   shield   donkey

Follow the directions in each sentence. Choose words from the box.

movie   reach   cookie   monkey   sweet   feet   beach

1. Write two words that rhyme with *peach.*

    reach   beach

2. Circle the way long *e* is spelled in the words you wrote.   ee (ea) ie ey

3. Change the first letter of *donkey*. Write a word from the box.

    monkey

4. Circle the way long *e* is spelled in the word you wrote.   ee ea ie (ey)

5. Write a word for a treat to eat with milk.   cookie

6. Circle the way long *e* is spelled in the word you wrote.   ee ea (ie) ey

7. Write two words that rhyme with *meet.*

    sweet   feet

8. Circle the way long *e* is spelled in the words you wrote.   (ee) ea ie ey

9. Write a word for what you see on a video.

    movie

10. Circle the way long *e* is spelled in the word you wrote.   ee ea (ie) ey

Notes for Home: Your child wrote words with different spellings for the long *e* sound. **Home Activity:** Look through a newspaper together to find words with long *e* spelled *ee, ea, ie,* or *ey*. Circle the words as you find them.

11

Name_____

The long *e* sound can be spelled *y* or *e.*

busy   me

Underline the words with the long *e* sound spelled *y*. Circle the words with the long *e* sound spelled *e*.

1. excitely   2. (she)   3. (zebra)

4. buggy   5. ugly   6. (we)

7. funny   8. (maybe)   9. everybody

Read each sentence. Change the underlined word or words to a word from above. Write the word.

10. Jake had a dog that was <u>not pretty</u>.

    ugly

11. Everyone thought Jake's dog, Muttsy, was <u>odd</u> looking.

    funny

12. When people laughed at her, <u>Muttsy</u> would bark at them.

    she

13. One day Muttsy showed <u>all Jake's friends</u> what a good dog she was.

    everybody

14. Muttsy kept a baby <u>carriage</u> from rolling into the street.

    buggy

15. Then all the people cheered <u>frantically</u>.

    excitedly

Notes for Home: Your child wrote words in which the long *e* sound is spelled *y* and *e*. **Home Activity:** Together with your child tell a story about a dog. Use some of the long *e* words from the page.

12

Answers **153**

The long *e* sound can be spelled in many different ways.

ee	as in	feet	ey	as in	valley
ea	as in	seat	y	as in	any
ie	as in	field	e	as in	we

Follow the long *e* path. In each box, underline two words with the long *e* sound. Circle the letter or letters that stand for the sound.

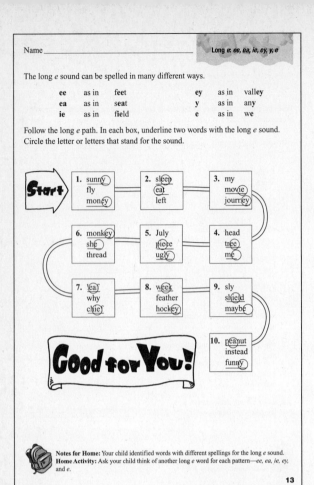

Start

1. sunny
   fly
   money

2. sleep
   eat
   left

3. my
   movie
   journey

6. monkey
   she
   thread

5. July
   piece
   ugly

4. head
   tree
   me

7. eat
   why
   chief

8. week
   feather
   hockey

9. sly
   shield
   maybe

10. peanut
    instead
    funny

Good for You!

Notes for Home: Your child identified words with different spellings for the long *e* sound. Home Activity: Ask your child think of another long *e* word for each pattern—*ee, ea, ie, ey,* and *e*.

13

Double consonants may come in the middle or at the end of words. The two letters usually stand for one sound.

    kitten   mirror   stuff   sell

Underline the word that completes each sentence and has double consonants.

1. Each morning you must ___.	eat	<u>dress</u>	wash
2. At the beach you might pick up a ___.	<u>shell</u>	crab	fish
3. An iron is used to ___ clothes.	wrinkle	heat	<u>press</u>
4. When writing, be sure to ___ correctly.	write	print	<u>spell</u>
5. One cent is also called a ___.	<u>penny</u>	coin	dollar
6. If something is small, it might be called ___.	wee	tiny	<u>little</u>
7. A special kind of church is called a ___.	place	<u>mission</u>	building
8. A thief is also called a ___.	burglar	<u>robber</u>	crook
9. The sound a turkey makes is called a ___.	cheep	cluck	<u>gobble</u>
10. We had tacos for ___.	breakfast	lunch	<u>dinner</u>

Notes for Home: Your child identified words with double consonants in the middle or at the end. Home Activity: Have your child read the underlined words and write another sentence for each one.

14

Words may have double consonants in the middle as in the word *muffin* or at the end as in the word *still*. The two consonants stand for one sound.

Follow each set of directions. Use the words in the box.

scissors	pretty	sheriff	call	full
cliff	pillow	dollar	fuzz	little

Write two words that end like *bell*.

1. call
2. full

Write two words that have two *t*'s in the middle like *kitten*.

3. pretty
4. little

Write two words that have two *l*'s like the word *follow*.

5. pillow
6. dollar

Write two words that end like *stuff*.

7. sheriff
8. cliff

Write another word with two *s*'s in the middle like the word *mission*.

9. scissors

Write another word that ends like *jazz*.

10. fuzz

Notes for Home: Your child identified and wrote words with double consonants in the middle and at the end. Home Activity: With your child, look through a favorite book. Take turns pointing to and naming other words with double consonants.

15

The letters *ai* and *ay* stand for the long *a* vowel sound.

    wait   **day**

Write each word in the box under the picture whose name has the same pattern for long *a* as the word.

gray	drain	paid	trail	way
stay	braid	rain	play	snail
paint	today	may	train	hay

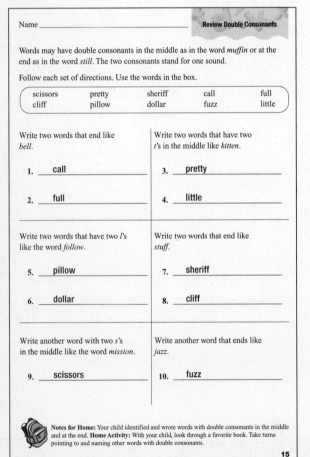

1. paint
2. drain
3. braid
4. paid
5. rain
6. trail
7. train
8. snail

9. gray
10. stay
11. today
12. may
13. play
14. way
15. hay

Notes for Home: Your child wrote words in which the long *a* sound is spelled *ai* or *ay*. Home Activity: Together use pairs of words from the box to make up rhymes.

16

Worksheet 17 (left top)

Name _____

The letters *oa*, *ow*, and *o* stand for the long *o* sound.

boat   show   go

Write the letter or letters that stand for the long *o* sound in each word. Then use the words to complete the ads.

1. coat **oa**

2. bowl **ow**

3. gold **o**

4. go **o**

5. soap **oa**

6. groan **oa**

7. mow **ow**

8. auto **o**

9. throat **oa**

10. snow **ow**

11. ON SALE TODAY! Beautiful Gold **Necklaces**

12. Come to TONY'S for a **bowl** of tasty Spaghetti

13. Does Your **Auto** Need New Brakes? Go to SALLY'S Repair Shop

14. Do You Have a Sore **Throat**? Dr. Lau Can Help

15. Need Your Grass Cut? I **Mow** Lawns! Call Me at 555-1814

Notes for Home: Your child wrote words in which the long *o* sound is spelled *oa*, *ow*, or *o*.
Home Activity: With your child, look at some newspaper ads. Try to find words with long *o* spelled *oa*, *ow*, or *o*.

17

Worksheet 18 (right top)

Name _____

The long *a* sound can be spelled *ai* and *ay*.   rain   hay
The long *o* sound can be spelled *oa*, *ow*, and *o*.   boat   show   gold

Find the word in each sentence that has the long *a* or long *o* sound. Write the word and circle the letters that stand for the long *a* or long *o* vowel sound.

1. A long time ago there lived a prince. **ago**

2. He had a pet goat called Rufus. **goat**

3. Rufus liked to play in the queen's garden. **play**

4. He would sneak in and slowly eat all the flowers. **slowly**

5. The prince would groan when he saw what Rufus had done. **groan**

6. One day the prince had a plan. **day**

7. He could not wait to try his idea. **wait**

8. So the prince led Rufus to the big front lawn. **So**

9. When Rufus saw all the dandelions, he wiggled his tail happily. **tail**

10. Now Rufus is the best lawn mower for the palace. **mower**

Notes for Home: Your child identified and wrote words with the long *a* and *o* vowel sounds.
Home Activity: With your child, tell another story about the prince and the goat. Use long *a* and long *o* words.

18

Worksheet 19 (left bottom)

Name _____

Sheet, teacher, field, and *money* have the long *e* sound.

sheet   teacher   field   money

Write only the words and phrases that have the long *e* sound in the camping trip list.

money	sunscreen	peaches	meat
bread	pieces of rope	clean clothes	sweets
field glasses	matches	sweaters	donkeys
extra eggs	canteens	honey	thread
peanut butter	sleeping bags	handkerchiefs	cookies

Camping Trip List

1. **money**
2. **field glasses**
3. **peanut butter**
4. **sunscreen**
5. **pieces of rope**
6. **canteens**
7. **sleeping bags**
8. **peaches**
9. **clean clothes**
10. **honey**
11. **handkerchiefs**
12. **meat**
13. **sweets**
14. **donkeys**
15. **cookies**

Notes for Home: Your child identified and wrote words with the long *e* sound.
Home Activity: Together look at the things written on the list. Talk about what the campers might do with each thing.

19

Worksheet 20 (right bottom)

Name _____

The long *e* sound can be spelled *y* as in *hungry* or *e* as in *she*.

Underline the words in each box that have the long *e* sound. Then rewrite each sentence. Use a word from the box in place of the underlined word or words.

1. they   2. we   3. she   4. he

5. What did Keesha tell you about the party?

   What did she tell you about the party?

6. Dave and I are planning to go early.

   We are planning to go early.

7. reply   8. tasty   9. many   10. funny   11. windy   12. why

13. There were lots of people at the party.

   There were many people at the party.

14. All the food was good.

   All the food was tasty.

15. Jerry told silly stories.

   Jerry told funny stories.

Notes for Home: Your child identified words with the long *e* sound. **Home Activity:** Talk with your child about a party that was fun. Name words with the long *e* sound that you use in your conversation.

20

Answers **155**

Worksheet 1 (page 21)

Name _____

The long i sound can be spelled *igh* and *y*.

       might   **my**

Write the answer to each clue and underline the letter or letters that stand for the long i sound.

| light | sight | sky | tight | right |
| cry | thigh | reply | fry | fly |

1. birds do this   **fly**
2. where to see stars   **sky**
3. one of the five senses   **sight**
4. the opposite of *left*   **right**
5. babies do this when hungry   **cry**
6. a lamp will give you this   **light**
7. to cook in oil   **fry**
8. part of your leg   **thigh**
9. to answer a question   **reply**
10. the opposite of *loose*   **tight**

Notes for Home: Your child wrote words in which the long i sound is spelled *igh* or *y*. **Home Activity:** Take turns with your child choosing a word from the list on the page and naming a rhyming word.

21

Worksheet 2 (page 22)

Name _____

The long u sound can be spelled u-consonant-e or u.

       fuse   **music**

Write the word that belongs in each group of words. Then underline the pattern that spells the long u sound in the word.

| January | united | huge | Utah | amuse |
| mule | cube | humorous | pupil | cute |

1. March, July, December, **January**   u-consonant-e   <u>u</u>
2. big, large, tremendous, **huge**   u-consonant-e   u
3. horse, zebra, donkey, **mule**   u-consonant-e   u
4. Illinois, Florida, Texas, **Utah**   u-consonant-e   <u>u</u>
5. learner, scholar, student, **pupil**   u-consonant-e   <u>u</u>
6. funny, silly, amusing, **humorous**   u-consonant-e   <u>u</u>
7. rectangle, circle, pyramid, **cube**   u-consonant-e   u
8. delight, entertain, raise a smile, **amuse**   u-consonant-e   u
9. cuddly, adorable, sweet, **cute**   u-consonant-e   u
10. joined, together, one, **united**   u-consonant-e   <u>u</u>

Notes for Home: Your child wrote words in which the long u sound is spelled u-consonant-e or u. **Home Activity:** Take turns with your child choosing a word he or she wrote on the page and giving a descriptive sentence for it.

22

Worksheet 3 (page 23)

Name _____

The long i sound can be spelled *igh* and *y*.   **tight**   **by**
The long u sound can be spelled u-consonant-e and u.   **fuse**   **human**

Write the words on the elephants in the correct lists.

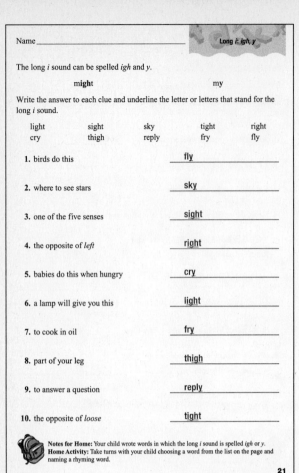

cube mute reply bright night future my amuse

cute menu sky humor sigh right uniform

music fly apply use light

Long i Spelled igh

1. **bright**
2. **night**
3. **sigh**
4. **right**
5. **light**

Long i Spelled y

6. **reply**
7. **my**
8. **sky**
9. **fly**
10. **apply**

Long u Spelled u-consonant-e

11. **cube**
12. **mute**
13. **cute**
14. **amuse**
15. **use**

Long u Spelled u

16. **future**
17. **menu**
18. **humor**
19. **music**
20. **uniform**

Notes for Home: Your child wrote words with the long i and long u sounds. **Home Activity:** Ask your child to add at least one more word to each list.

23

Worksheet 4 (page 24)

Name _____

The letters *a*, *e*, *i*, *o*, and *u* stand for short vowel sounds.

  bat   bed   sit   hot   cut

Say each picture name. Write **Yes** if the word has a short vowel sound. Then write the letter that stands for the short vowel sound. Write **No** if the word does not have a short vowel sound.

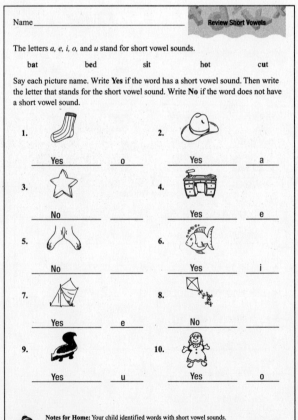

1. **Yes**   **o**
2. **Yes**   **a**
3. **No**
4. **Yes**   **e**
5. **No**
6. **Yes**   **i**
7. **Yes**   **e**
8. **No**
9. **Yes**   **u**
10. **Yes**   **o**

Notes for Home: Your child identified words with short vowel sounds. **Home Activity:** Have your child cut out magazine pictures whose names have short vowel sounds, paste the pictures on paper, and write the letters that stand for the short vowel sounds in the picture names.

24

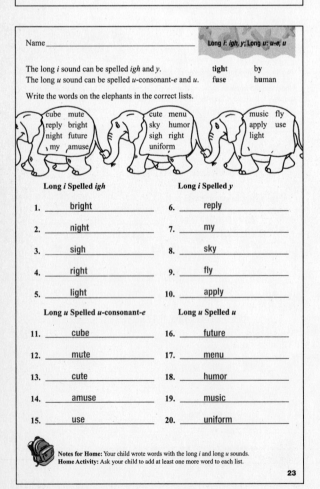

Name_____   Review Short Vowels

Some words have short vowel sounds.

a	e	i	o	u
hat	ten	dish	hot	cup

Write the word that answers the question. Underline the letter that stands for the short vowel sound in the word.

1. If you were hot, would you use a jet, a mop, or a fan to get cool?   f<u>a</u>n

2. Does a mitt, a hand, or a lid cover a pot?   l<u>i</u>d

3. Would you wear a cap, a vest, or a muff on your head?   c<u>a</u>p

4. Would you ride on a bat, a bus, or a box?   b<u>u</u>s

5. What would you use to clean up a spill—a rug, a mitt, or a mop?   m<u>o</u>p

6. Would you see a sled, a shell, or a bib on a turtle?   sh<u>e</u>ll

7. Can a bat, a pig, or a pup fly?   b<u>a</u>t

8. Is a cat, a hen, or a fox a bird?   h<u>e</u>n

9. Would a cup, a cut, or a cot need a bandage?   c<u>u</u>t

10. Would you swim, run, or hop across a pond?   sw<u>i</u>m

Notes for Home: Your child identified and wrote words with short vowel sounds.
Home Activity: Take turns with your child asking questions like those on the page. Use words with short vowel sounds as choices for the answers.

25

Name_____   Compound Words

A compound word is made up of two words.

air + plane = airplane

Draw lines to match words that make compound words. Write the compound words.

1. foot — ball   football
2. rain — coat   raincoat
3. pop — corn   popcorn

4. hand — stand   handstand
5. ear — ring   earring
6. bird — house   birdhouse

7. gold — fish   goldfish
8. paint — brush   paintbrush
9. drum — stick   drumstick
10. news — paper   newspaper

Notes for Home: Your child joined words to make and write compound words.
Home Activity: Write each small word on the page on a piece of scrap paper. Have your child match the papers to form compound words.

26

Name_____   Compound Words

A compound word is made of two smaller words.

when + ever = whenever   left + over = leftover

Underline the compound word that completes the sentence. Then draw a line between the words that make up the compound word.

1. One spring morning after ___, Mom called to me.   sunset / break<u>|</u>fast

2. She said we could plant some ___ in the garden.   raindrops / sun<u>|</u>flowers

3. We went ___ into the backyard where we have a garden.   out<u>|</u>side / inside

4. ___ she turned over some dirt with a shovel, I saw worms.   However / When<u>|</u>ever

5. ___ I had to pull up some big clumps of weeds.   Some<u>|</u>times / Anytime

6. Sparrows peeked out of the ___ and watched us dig.   bedroom / bird<u>|</u>house

7. We knew that in time ___ beautiful would grow.   someone / some<u>|</u>thing

8. We sprinkled seeds on the soil, and then we pushed the seeds ___ the soil with a rake.   in<u>|</u>to / onto

9. As a last step, we poured some ___ over the soil.   buttermilk / rain<u>|</u>water

10. In the ___, we spend a lot of time working in our garden.   wintertime / summer<u>|</u>time

Notes for Home: Your child identified the words that make up compound words.
Home Activity: Have your child continue the story by telling what happened after the sunflowers grew. Point out any compound words your child uses.

27

Name_____   Review Long i: igh, y

The letters igh and y stand for the long i sound in tight and cry.

Follow each direction.

1. Write fly. Circle the letter that spells the long i sound.   fl(y)

2. Change f to s. Write the new word.   sly

3. Change l to k. Write the new word.   sky

4. Change k to h. Write the new word.   shy

5. Change s to w. Write the new word.   why

6. Write sigh. Circle the letters that spell the long i sound.   s(igh)

7. Add a t at the end. Write the new word.   sight

8. Change s to t. Write the new word.   tight

9. Change the first t to n. Write the new word.   night

10. Add a k at the beginning. Write the new word.   knight

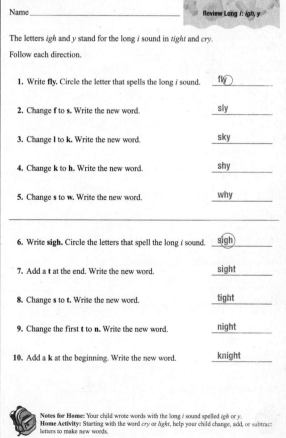

Notes for Home: Your child wrote words with the long i sound spelled igh or y.
Home Activity: Starting with the word cry or light, help your child change, add, or subtract letters to make new words.

28

Answers 157

Page 29

Name _____

The long *u* sound can be spelled *u*-consonant-*e* or *u*.

cute   **unit**

Denzel has to find all the words with long *u* spelled *u*-consonant-*e*. Maria has to find all the words with long *u* spelled *u*. Write the words in the correct lists. Not all the words will be used.

music	humor	use	future	mule
sum	amuse	pull	cube	cuteness
fuse	uniform	useful	menu	pupil
number	put	curl	push	burn
must	bush	human	huge	turtle

Denzel's List

1. fuse
2. amuse
3. use
4. useful
5. cube
6. huge
7. mule
8. cuteness

Maria's List

9. music
10. humor
11. uniform
12. human
13. future
14. menu
15. pupil

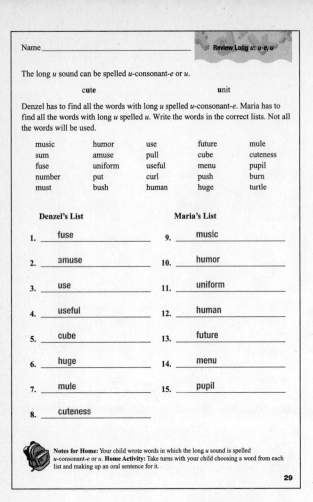

Notes for Home: Your child wrote words in which the long *u* sound is spelled *u*-consonant-*e* or *u*. **Home Activity:** Take turns with your child choosing a word from each list and making up an oral sentence for it.

29

Page 30

Name _____

The long *i* sound can be spelled *igh* and *y*.   **right**   **fly**

The long *u* sound can be spelled *u*-consonant-*e* and *u*.   **use**   **menu**

Write *i* or *u* to tell what long vowel sound you hear in each word. Then circle the pattern that spells the long vowel sound.

Word	Vowel Sound Heard	How Is It Spelled?
1. mule	u	*igh* *y* (*u*-consonant-*e*) *u*
2. apply	i	*igh* (*y*) *u*-consonant-*e* *u*
3. high	i	(*igh*) *y* *u*-consonant-*e* *u*
4. flying	i	*igh* (*y*) *u*-consonant-*e* *u*
5. music	u	*igh* *y* *u*-consonant-*e* (*u*)
6. tighter	i	(*igh*) *y* *u*-consonant-*e* *u*
7. unit	u	*igh* *y* *u*-consonant-*e* (*u*)
8. cube	u	*igh* *y* (*u*-consonant-*e*) *u*
9. myself	i	*igh* (*y*) *u*-consonant-*e* *u*
10. amuse	u	*igh* *y* (*u*-consonant-*e*) *u*

Notes for Home: Your child identified the spelling patterns in long *i* and long *u* words. **Home Activity:** Help your child list other long *i* and long *u* words. Ask your child what long vowel sound is heard in each word.

30

Page 31

Name _____

The letters *oo* stand for the vowel sounds in these words.

boot   **good**

Write each word under the word that has the same vowel sound.

| book | foot | hoot | hood | zoo |
| moon | spoon | hook | broom | wood |

soon

1. moon
2. spoon
3. hoot
4. broom
5. zoo

look

6. book
7. foot
8. hook
9. hood
10. wood

Write a word from above that answers each clue.

11. Eat soup with this.   spoon

12. Catch fish on this.   hook

13. Owls do this.   hoot

14. Sweep the floor with this.   broom

15. A jacket might have this.   hood

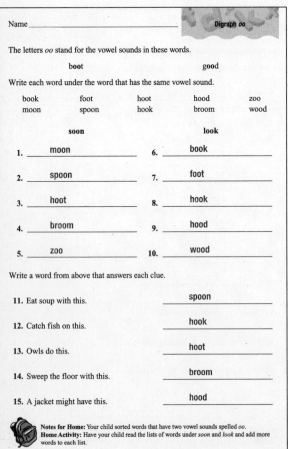

Notes for Home: Your child sorted words that have two vowel sounds spelled *oo*. **Home Activity:** Have your child read the lists of words under *soon* and *look* and add more words to each list.

31

Page 32

Name _____

The letters *oo* stand for the vowel sound in *look*.
The letters *oo* also stand for the vowel sound in *too*.

Unscramble the letters to make words from the list. Write the letters on the lines. Underline the word at the right that has the same vowel sound as the word you made.

| hook | fool | moon | boot | good |
| wood | goose | hood | school | |

1. oogse	g o o s e (1)	look	cool
2. koco	c o o k (2)	hook	zoo
3. ohod	h o o d (3)	cookie	spool
4. tboo	b o o t (4)	brook	loose
5. oodw	w o o d (5)	took	noodle
6. cosolh	s c h o o l (6)	shook	pool
7. borom	b r o o m (7)	wool	room
8. ogdo	g o o d (8)	book	noon
9. nomo	m o o n (10)	stood	balloon

Write the numbered letters to answer the riddle.

Where is a place to learn?

10. s c h o o l r o o m
     1 2 3 4 5 6 7 8 9 10

Notes for Home: Your child identified words with the *oo* vowel pattern. **Home Activity:** List some other words with *oo*. Take turns with your child scrambling the words and having the other person write them correctly.

32

---

158 Answers

In *book*, the vowel sound is spelled *oo*.
In *noon*, the vowel sound is spelled *oo*.

Underline the word that has the same vowel sound as the picture name.

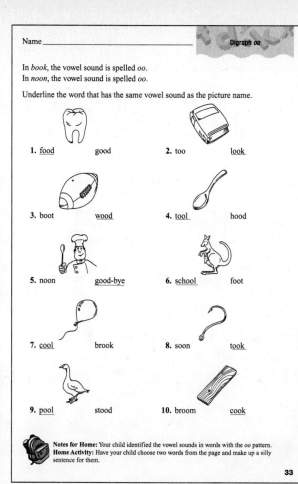

1. <u>food</u>   good

2. too   <u>look</u>

3. boot   <u>wood</u>

4. <u>tool</u>   hood

5. noon   <u>good-bye</u>

6. <u>school</u>   foot

7. <u>cool</u>   brook

8. soon   <u>took</u>

9. <u>pool</u>   stood

10. broom   <u>cook</u>

Notes for Home: Your child identified the vowel sounds in words with the *oo* pattern.
Home Activity: Have your child choose two words from the page and make up a silly sentence for them.

33

A compound word is made from two smaller words.

back + yard = backyard   any + body = anybody

Underline two words in each sentence that can be put together to make a compound word. Write the word.

1. I went <u>up</u> to the second floor using the <u>stairs</u>.   upstairs

2. For a trip in <u>space</u>, you will need a <u>ship</u>.   spaceship

3. He went <u>out</u> and played along the <u>side</u> of the house.   outside

4. She bought <u>some</u> toys but not another <u>thing</u>.   something

5. The <u>air</u> in the <u>plane</u> was hot and stuffy.   airplane

6. The <u>bed</u> in her <u>room</u> had not been made.   bedroom

7. A bright <u>moon</u> gave us <u>light</u> to see by.   moonlight

8. Did you see the <u>sun</u> as it <u>set</u> last evening?   sunset

9. There was a lot of <u>news</u> in today's <u>paper</u>.   newspaper

10. Put the baby into the <u>seat</u> and fasten the <u>belt</u>.   seatbelt

Notes for Home: Your child combined words to make compound words.
Home Activity: Take turns with your child writing the first part of a compound word on a piece of paper and having the other person write the second part of the compound word.

34

A compound word is made up of two words put together.

in + to = into   any + body = anybody

Draw lines to match words to make compound words. Then write the compound words under the heading that tells about them.

1. foot — plane
2. out — ball
3. air — yard
4. pop — side
5. back — corn

6. rail — ground
7. basket — ball
8. play — ship
9. space — berries
10. straw — road

Sports
11. football
12. basketball

Food
13. popcorn
14. strawberries

Places
15. outside
16. backyard
17. playground

Ways to Travel
18. airplane
19. railroad
20. spaceship

Notes for Home: Your child formed and classified compound words.
Home Activity: Together name other compound words. Think of a category name for each compound.

35

The letters *ou* stand for the vowel sounds in these words.

cloud   couple   boulder   would   soup

Write an *ou* word from the box that rhymes with the underlined word.

| double | you | ground | touch | group |
| house | should | shoulder | could | pounce |

1. See what I <u>found</u> lying on the ___ground___.

2. Did you see a <u>mouse</u> in the basement of your ___house___?

3. I hope you made enough <u>soup</u> to feed the whole ___group___.

4. Each time the ball would <u>bounce</u>, the cat would ___pounce___.

5. If you water the plant too <u>much</u>, it will be too wet to ___touch___.

6. If I had a saw, I ___could___ cut this great big piece of <u>wood</u>.

7. I cannot come to visit ___you___ because today I have the <u>flu</u>.

8. They moved the <u>boulder</u> off the road and onto the ___shoulder___.

9. Whenever Dave is in <u>trouble</u>, he wishes he had a ___double___.

10. To keep my ears warm, I ___should___ pull up my jacket <u>hood</u>.

Notes for Home: Your child identified words with the *ou* vowel pattern.
Home Activity: Have your child look in a newspaper, find *ou* words, and name rhyming words.

36

Worksheet 37

Name_____ **Digraph *ou* and Diphthong *ou***

The letters *ou* stand for the vowel sounds in these words.

cloud   touch   boulder   would   you

Write each word in the box under the word that has the same vowel sound for *ou*.

should	young	could	shoulder	house
mouse	shout	country	soup	couple
double	group	loud	trouble	ground

ou as in *cloud*

1. mouse
2. shout
3. loud
4. house
5. ground

ou as in *touch*

6. double
7. young
8. country
9. trouble
10. couple

ou as in *would*

11. should
12. could

ou as in *you*

13. group
14. soup

ou as in *boulder*

15. shoulder

Notes for Home: Your child grouped words according to their vowel sounds spelled *ou*.
Home Activity: Choose a word from the box and use it to begin a story. Ask your child to choose other words and use them to add to the story.

37

Worksheet 38

Name_____ **Digraph *ou* and Diphthong *ou***

The letters *ou* stand for the vowel sounds in these words.

ground   should   you   double   boulder

Write each word next to a word that has the same vowel sound.

about   you   could
1. would _could_
2. youth _you_
3. sound _about_

mouse   soup   poultry
4. ground _mouse_
5. shoulder _poultry_
6. toucan _soup_

should   couple
7. young _couple_
8. could _should_

trouble   cloud
9. about _cloud_
10. touch _trouble_

Notes for Home: Your child wrote words with the *ou* vowel pattern.
Home Activity: Take turns with your child choosing two words from one of the boxes and making up a sentence with the two words.

38

Worksheet 39

Name_____ **Review Digraph *oo***

The letters *oo* stand for the vowel sounds in *spoon* and *foot*.

Write each word in the box under the picture whose name has the same vowel sound as the word.

tooth	look	wood	moose	loop
hood	boot	moon	school	took
spool	cook	hook	book	stool
stood	shook	good	goose	zoo

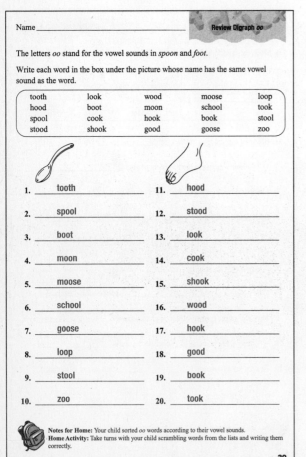

1. tooth
2. spool
3. boot
4. moon
5. moose
6. school
7. goose
8. loop
9. stool
10. zoo

11. hood
12. stood
13. look
14. cook
15. shook
16. wood
17. hook
18. good
19. book
20. took

Notes for Home: Your child sorted *oo* words according to their vowel sounds.
Home Activity: Take turns with your child scrambling words from the lists and writing them correctly.

39

Worksheet 40

Name_____ **Review Digraph *oo***

The letters *oo* stand for the vowel sounds in *room* and *foot*.

Underline the words that have the same vowel sound as the word in dark type. Then write the underlined word that goes with each clue.

room
1. moon   2. boots   3. look   4. stood   5. school
6. shook   7. wood   8. shoots   9. tools   10. took

11. what cowhands wear on their feet — boots
12. a hammer, saw, and wrench — tools
13. something seen in the night sky — moon
14. what a player does with a basketball — shoots
15. a place where children learn — school

took
16. choose   17. mood   18. foot   19. wood   20. loose
21. hook   22. soon   23. books   24. moose   25. hood

26. a place to hang a coat — hook
27. what some furniture is made of — wood
28. something on a jacket — hood
29. something at the end of a leg — foot
30. what you would see in a library — books

Notes for Home: Your child wrote words with the *oo* vowel pattern. **Home Activity:** Take turns with your child choosing a word from a list and naming words that rhyme with it.

40

The letter *j* stands for /j/ in *just*.
The letter *g* stands for /j/ in *gem*.

Underline the word in each sentence that has /j/. Circle the letter that spells /j/.

1. Did you read that <u>page</u>? j **(g)**

2. <u>Giraffes</u> have long necks. j **(g)**

3. A kangaroo can <u>jump</u>. **(j)** g

4. A <u>jungle</u> has many trees. **(j)** g

5. Do you <u>enjoy</u> singing? **(j)** g

6. Be <u>gentle</u> with pets. j **(g)**

7. Read about a <u>giant</u> in a story. j **(g)**

8. The first month is <u>January</u>. **(j)** g

9. Let's study about <u>Jupiter</u>. **(j)** g

10. They have a <u>large</u> cat. j **(g)**

Notes for Home: Your child identified words in which /j/ is spelled *j* or *g*.
Home Activity: Ask your child to make a sentence in which one word has /j/ spelled *j* or *g*.

41

The letter *s* stands for /s/ in *safe*.
The letter *c* stands for /s/ in *ice*.

Read each word. Circle **Yes** if you hear /s/. Circle **No** if you do not.

1. city **(Yes)** No
2. side **(Yes)** No
3. can Yes **(No)**

4. some **(Yes)** No
5. face **(Yes)** No
6. does Yes **(No)**

7. mice **(Yes)** No
8. call Yes **(No)**
9. once **(Yes)** No

10. please Yes **(No)**
11. center **(Yes)** No
12. bus **(Yes)** No

13. cent **(Yes)** No
14. summer **(Yes)** No
15. place **(Yes)** No

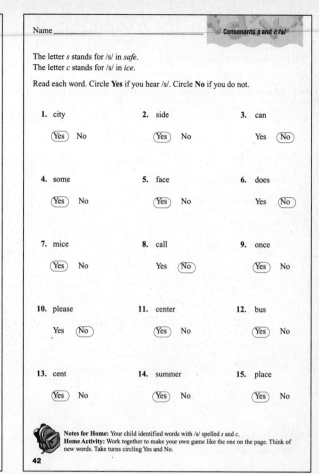

Notes for Home: Your child identified words with /s/ spelled *s* and *c*.
Home Activity: Work together to make your own game like the one on the page. Think of new words. Take turns circling Yes and No.

42

Name _____ Consonants *j* and *g* /j/;
Consonants *s* and *c* /s/

The letters *j* and *g* can spell the *j* sound. **jump** **giant**
The letters *s* and *c* can spell the *s* sound. **side** **rice**

Underline the words in the box that have /j/ spelled *j* or *g* or that have /s/ spelled *s* or *c*. Write the words you underline in ABC order.

1. <u>joy</u>	2. <u>giraffe</u>	3. <u>page</u>	4. goat	5. <u>base</u>
6. <u>ice</u>	7. cook	8. <u>sent</u>	9. <u>gentle</u>	10. <u>jeep</u>
11. was	12. <u>race</u>	13. cup	14. <u>mice</u>	15. <u>gem</u>
16. <u>some</u>	17. <u>edge</u>	18. cat	19. <u>safe</u>	20. <u>city</u>

ABC Order

21. base
22. city
23. edge
24. gem
25. gentle
26. giraffe
27. ice
28. jeep
29. joy
30. mice
31. page
32. race
33. safe
34. sent
35. some

Notes for Home: Your child identified words in which *j* or *g* spelled /j/ and *s* or *c* spelled /s/.
Home Activity: Have your child choose three words with /j/ and /s/ from a book or magazine and write the words in ABC order.

43

Name _____ Review Long *a*: *ai*, *ay*

The letters *ai* and *ay* can spell the long *a* sound.

hail **day**

Write *ai* or *ay* to make the words in the list.

tray mail train May
stay brain rain away

1. r <u>a</u> <u>i</u> n
2. aw <u>a</u> <u>y</u>
3. br <u>a</u> <u>i</u> n
4. tr <u>a</u> <u>i</u> n
5. st <u>a</u> <u>y</u>
6. M <u>a</u> <u>y</u>
7. m <u>a</u> <u>i</u> l
8. tr <u>a</u> <u>y</u>

Write a word from above that answers each clue.

9. This is wet and falls in drops. rain
10. An engine and cars make up this. train
11. If you do not leave, you do this. stay
12. This is the month after April. May
13. A package might be called this. mail
14. You carry things on this. tray
15. You think with this. brain

Notes for Home: Your child identified and wrote words with long *a* spelled *ai* and *ay*.
Home Activity: Have your child find and circle words in a newspaper in which long *a* is spelled *ai* or *ay*.

44

Answers **161**

Name_____

The letters *oa*, *ow*, and *o* stand for the long *o* sound.

      boat   **show**   **most**

Put each sentence in the correct order. Circle two words with the long *o* sound.

1. The old is radio. The (radio) is (old.)

2. wore a coat one No. (No) one wore a (coat.)

3. this down Go road. (Go) down this (road.)

4. soap Does the float? Does the (soap) (float?)

5. throat My is sore so. My (throat) is (so) sore.

6. coach is hero The a. The (coach) is a (hero.)

7. a toad a song Can croak? Can a (toad) (croak) a song?

8. is mowed The lawn almost.

    The lawn is (almost) (mowed.)

9. along the coast walked slowly We.

    We walked (slowly) along the (coast.)

10. poem The does not about snow rhyme.

    The (poem) about (snow) does not rhyme.

Notes for Home: Your child identified words with the long *o* sound spelled *oa*, *ow*, and *o*.
Home Activity: Have your child make up other sentences that have at least one word with the long *o* sound.

45

Name_____

The letters *ow* stand for the vowel sounds in these words.

      grow   **how**

Write words from the box to complete the phrases.

down	throw	window	now	town
snow	below	shower	slow	frown

1. not up, but ____ down ____   2. not door, but ____ window ____

3. not above, but ____ below ____   4. not catch, but ____ throw ____

5. not later, but ____ now ____   6. not rain, but ____ snow ____

7. not fast, but ____ slow ____   8. not bath, but ____ shower ____

9. not smile, but ____ frown ____   10. not city, but ____ town ____

Write each word in the box under the word that has the same vowel sound.

      grow   **clown**

11. ____ snow ____   16. ____ down ____

12. ____ throw ____   17. ____ shower ____

13. ____ below ____   18. ____ now ____

14. ____ window ____   19. ____ town ____

15. ____ slow ____   20. ____ frown ____

Notes for Home: Your child wrote words with the *ow* vowel pattern.
Home Activity: Take turns with your child naming a word on the page and then pointing to and naming another word on the page with the same vowel sound.

46

Name_____

The letters *ow* stand for the vowel sounds in *grow* and *how*.

Write the word that goes with the picture. Circle the letters that stand for the vowel sound in *grow* or *how*.

clown	shower	crowd	crown	arrow
row	shadow	howl	crow	pillow

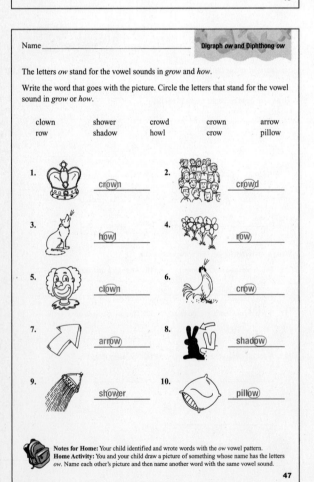

1. cr(ow)n   2. cr(ow)d

3. h(ow)l   4. r(ow)

5. cl(ow)n   6. cr(ow)

7. arr(ow)   8. shad(ow)

9. sh(ow)er   10. pill(ow)

Notes for Home: Your child identified and wrote words with the *ow* vowel pattern.
Home Activity: You and your child draw a picture of something whose name has the letters *ow*. Name each other's picture and then name another word with the same vowel sound.

47

Name_____

The letters *ow* stand for the vowel sounds in these words.

      clown   **below**

Follow the directions. Write the new words. Then circle the answer to the question.

1. **blow**   Change **bl** to **gr**.   ____ grow ____

           Change **gr** to **cr**.   ____ crow ____

   Does *ow* stand for the same sound in each word you wrote?   (Yes)   No

2. **row**   Change **r** to **sn**.   ____ snow ____

           Change **sn** to **pl**.   ____ plow ____

   Does *ow* stand for the same sound in each word you wrote?   Yes   (No)

3. **know**   Change **kn** to **m**.   ____ mow ____

           Change **m** to **c**.   ____ cow ____

   Does *ow* stand for the same sound in each word you wrote?   Yes   (No)

4. **power**   Change **p** to **t**.   ____ tower ____

           Change **t** to **fl**.   ____ flower ____

   Does *ow* stand for the same sound in each word you wrote?   (Yes)   No

5. **yellow**   Change **ye** to **a**.   ____ allow ____

           Change **al** to **be**.   ____ below ____

   Does *ow* stand for the same sound in each word you wrote?   Yes   (No)

Notes for Home: Your child wrote words with the *ow* vowel pattern.
Home Activity: Starting with *down*, *snow*, or *crown*, help your child change letters to make new words.

48

The letters *j* and *g* can stand for /j/.   just   age

In each category, write the words that have the *j* sound spelled *j* or *g*.

Months

January **1.** _January_

June **2.** _June_

July **3.** _July_

August

Clothes

jacket **4.** _jacket_

jumper **5.** _jumper_

gloves **6.** _jeans_

jeans

Size

huge **7.** _huge_

big **8.** _jumbo_

jumbo **9.** _large_

large

Names

Ginger **10.** _Ginger_

Greg **11.** _Joel_

Joel **12.** _George_

George

Places

garden **13.** _Japan_

Japan **14.** _region_

region **15.** _village_

village

Notes for Home: Your child wrote words in which /j/ is spelled *j* or *g*.
Home Activity: Take turns with your child naming another word that belongs in each group and telling whether the word has /j/ spelled *j* or *g*.

49

The letters *s* and *c* can stand for /s/.   saw   race

Write the word that answers each clue. Circle the letter that stands for the *s* sound.

city   summer   mice   pencil   baseball
yes   sea   ceiling   cereal   soft

1. the top of a room   _ceiling_   s (c)

2. a season of the year   _summer_   (s) c

3. place where many people live   _city_   s (c)

4. the opposite of *no*   _yes_   (s) c

5. something to write with   _pencil_   s (c)

6. a large body of water   _sea_   (s) c

7. more than one mouse   _mice_   s (c)

8. something to eat in the morning   _cereal_   s (c)

9. the opposite of *hard*   _soft_   (s) c

10. a sport with a batter   _baseball_   (s) c

Notes for Home: Your child wrote words in which /s/ is spelled *s* or *c*.
Home Activity: Ask your child to think of other words that have /s/ spelled *s* or *c* and to make up meaning clues for the words.

50

In some pairs of letters, only one letter stands for a sound. The other letter is silent. Note the silent letter in each of these words.

wrench   **kn**ob   fas**t**en   desi**gn**   cli**mb**

Write the letter that is not heard in each word.

1. wren _w_   **2.** knot _k_

3. knew _k_   **4.** lamb _b_

5. sign _g_   **6.** wrap _w_

7. wrong _w_   **8.** assign _g_

9. comb _b_   **10.** listen _t_

Write the word that completes each sentence. Use words from above.

11. Mary had a little _lamb_.

12. She _knew_ it could not go to school with her.

13. It was _wrong_ for her pet to follow her.

14. She read the _sign_ that said, "No pets at school!"

15. But the animal would not _listen_ to her and stay at home.

Notes for Home: Your child identified words with silent letters. **Home Activity:** Have your child read sentences on the page. Discuss how Mary could solve her problem.

51

Each of these words has a silent letter—a letter that does not stand for a sound.

wrap   **kn**ot   fas**t**en   desi**gn**   com**b**

Write a rhyming word for each numbered word below.

write   sign   wreath   lamb   knuckle
knee   knit   thumb   reign   listen

1. fit _knit_   **2.** some _thumb_

3. night _write_   **4.** tree _knee_

5. mine _sign_   **6.** train _reign_

7. ham _lamb_   **8.** buckle _knuckle_

9. teeth _wreath_   **10.** glisten _listen_

Use the words you wrote above to answer these questions.

11. Which two words have a silent *w*?

write   _wreath_

12. Which three words have a silent *k*?

knit   _knee_   _knuckle_

13. Which word has a silent *t*? _listen_

14. Which two words have a silent *g*?

sign   _reign_

15. Which two words have a silent *b*?

lamb   _thumb_

Notes for Home: Your child identified silent letters in words. **Home Activity:** Have your child look through newspaper and magazine ads for other words with silent letters and then circle each word and tell what letter is silent.

52

Answers **163**

The letters *ou* stand for the vowel sounds in these words.

ground   should   **you**   touch   poultry

Write each word on the line with the matching number. Then underline the word that rhymes with the word you wrote.

(5) soup   (1) double   (9) mouth   (10) shout   (8) shoulder
(2) boulder   (4) would   (6) cloud   (3) round   (7) pouch

1. _____double_____   grouch   would   <u>trouble</u>

2. _____boulder_____   <u>shoulder</u>   younger   prouder

3. _____round_____   proud   <u>pound</u>   doubled

4. _____would_____   sound   counted   <u>could</u>

5. _____soup_____   shout   bounce   <u>group</u>

6. _____cloud_____   <u>crowd</u>   should   roughed

7. _____pouch_____   though   young   <u>couch</u>

8. _____shoulder_____   <u>boulder</u>   counter   tougher

9. _____mouth_____   fourth   <u>south</u>   count

10. _____shout_____   southern   <u>about</u>   thought

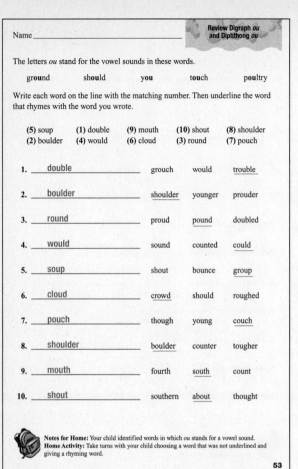

Notes for Home: Your child identified words in which *ou* stands for a vowel sound.
Home Activity: Take turns with your child choosing a word that was not underlined and giving a rhyming word.

53

Listen to the different sounds the letters *ou* can stand for.

sound   could   **you**   couple   shoulder

Put an X on the box if the letters *ou* stand for two different vowel sounds in the words.

1. about around H	2. should would W	3. toucan (X) scout G
4. double country O	5. proud (X) youth R	6. you soup A
7. mouth (X) group E	8. touch young F	9. loud noun I
10. house pound R	11. amount (X) trouble A	12. poultry boulder L
13. would (X) found T	14. cougar group H	15. double young D

Write the letters from the boxes with X's. There is a message for you.

   <u>G</u>   <u>R</u>   <u>E</u>   <u>A</u>   <u>T</u> !

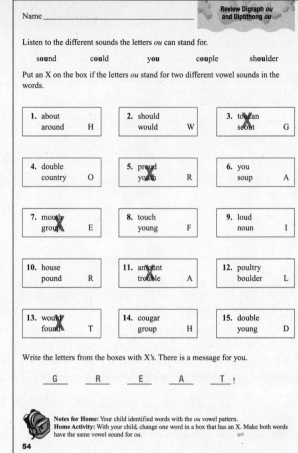

Notes for Home: Your child identified words with the *ou* vowel pattern.
Home Activity: With your child, change one word in a box that has an X. Make both words have the same vowel sound for *ou*.

54

In each of these words, the letters *ou* stand for a different vowel sound.

around   could   **you**   touch   shoulder

Change the words to make new words with the *ou* vowel pattern. Add and subtract letters. Write each new word.

1. mouse – se + th = _____mouth_____

2. group – gr + s = _____soup_____

3. should – ld + t = _____shout_____

4. pouch – ch + nd = _____pound_____

5. young – ng + th = _____youth_____

6. couch – ch + ld = _____could_____

7. fountain – f + m = _____mountain_____

8. boulder – b + sh = _____shoulder_____

9. toucan – an + h = _____touch_____

10. could – ld + nt = _____count_____

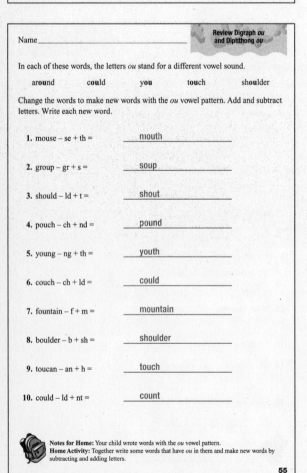

Notes for Home: Your child wrote words with the *ou* vowel pattern.
Home Activity: Together write some words that have *ou* in them and make new words by subtracting and adding letters.

55

The letters *ar* and *or* stand for the vowel sounds in these words.

farm   horn

Underline the word that has the same vowel sound as the picture name.

1.   cart   <u>cord</u>

2.   large   <u>horn</u>

3.   dark   <u>orbit</u>

4.   far   <u>store</u>

5.   <u>farm</u>   north

6.   card   <u>story</u>

7.   <u>yard</u>   force

8.   <u>park</u>   short

9.   bark   <u>more</u>

10.   <u>part</u>   fort

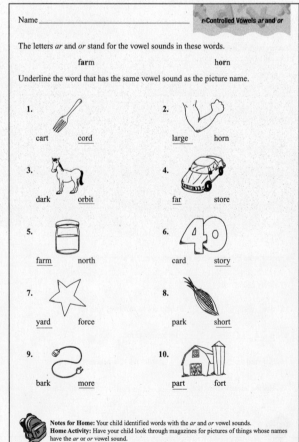

Notes for Home: Your child identified words with the *ar* and *or* vowel sounds.
Home Activity: Have your child look through magazines for pictures of things whose names have the *ar* or *or* vowel sound.

56

---

164   Answers

The letters *er, ir, or,* and *ur* stand for the vowel sound in these words.

her   bird   word   fur

Write the word in the sentence that has the vowel sound in *her, bird, word,* and *fur.*
Circle the letters that stand for the vowel sound.

1. A fern is a plant.   ____fern____   (er)   ir
                                                    or   ur

2. I have a burn on my hand.   ____burn____   er   ir
                                                    or   (ur)

3. Turtles walk slowly.   ____Turtles____   er   ir
                                                    or   (ur)

4. She won third prize.   ____third____   er   (ir)
                                                    or   ur

5. Draw a circle on the sidewalk. ____circle____   er   (ir)
                                                    or   ur

6. The poem has two verses.   ____verses____   (er)   ir
                                                    or   ur

7. Here is a world map.   ____world____   er   ir
                                                   (or)   ur

8. I want to be a nurse.   ____nurse____   er   ir
                                                    or   (ur)

9. The skirt touched the ground. ____skirt____   er   (ir)
                                                    or   ur

10. A worm is on the sidewalk. ____worm____   er   ir
                                                   (or)   ur

Notes for Home: Your child identified words with the *er, ir, or,* and *ur* vowel patterns.
Home Activity: Take turns with your child choosing a word written above. One person writes the word, leaving out two letters. The other person guesses the word and writes the missing letters.

57

The letters *air* and *are* stand for the vowel sound in these words.   hair care

The letters *ear* stand for the vowel sound in this word.   hear

Write each word in the box that has a word with the same vowel sound and the same spelling.

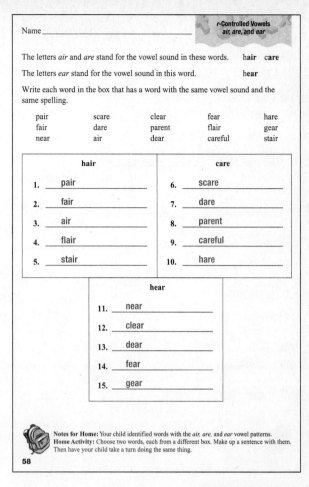

pair   scare   clear   fear   hare
fair   dare   parent   flair   gear
near   air   dear   careful   stair

hair		care	
1. pair		6. scare	
2. fair		7. dare	
3. air		8. parent	
4. flair		9. careful	
5. stair		10. hare	

hear	
11. near	
12. clear	
13. dear	
14. fear	
15. gear	

Notes for Home: Your child identified words with the *air, are,* and *ear* vowel patterns.
Home Activity: Choose two words, each from a different box. Make up a sentence with them. Then have your child take a turn doing the same thing.

58

The letters *ow* stand for the vowel sounds in *own* and *down.*

Draw a line from the word in the box to the word with the same vowel sound.

1. now — grow / growl / own

2. owe — show / scowl / power

3. town — low / mow / brown

4. bowl — vowel / cow / owner

5. crow — crowd / tower / flow

6. shower — throw / now / snow

7. powder — plow / mower / blow

8. slow — own / frown / powder

9. tow — flower / how / glow

10. crown — allow / stow / below

Notes for Home: Your child matched words with the same vowel sound spelled *ow.*
Home Activity: With one hand, point to a word on the page. With the other hand, point to another word with the same vowel sound. Then ask your child to take a turn.

59

The letters *ow* stand for the vowel sounds in *down* and *own.*

Write a word from the box that has the same vowel sound as the underlined word and completes the sentence.

town   slowly   grow   bowling   mow
growling vowel   throw   flower   towel

1. I _know_ it is time for me to ____mow____ the grass.

2. A large _crowd_ gathered in the ____town____ square.

3. The _clown_ had a ____flower____ that squirted water.

4. I would like to _own_ a red ____bowling____ ball.

5. The _snowman_ ____slowly____ melted in the warm sun.

6. After my _shower,_ I dried off with a ____towel____.

7. The man _scowled_ at the ____growling____ dog.

8. Will you _show_ me how to ____throw____ a football?

9. The _row_ of corn started to ____grow____ tall.

10. _Somehow_ I will learn all the ____vowel____ sounds.

Notes for Home: Your child wrote words with the *ow* vowel pattern.
Home Activity: Read two words from the box. Have your child tell if the two words have the same vowel sound. Then let your child read two words.

60

Answers **165**

Page 61

To find the base word, you must take off any prefixes, suffixes, or endings.

uncover   care**ful**   **search**es   re**build**ing

Add the prefixes, suffixes, or endings to the base words. Write the new word.

1. re + teach = _____reteach_____

2. pull + ing = _____pulling_____

3. re + fold + ed = _____refolded_____

4. dis + honest + ly = _____dishonestly_____

5. help + less + ness = _____helplessness_____

Write the base word for each word.

6. remake
_____make_____

7. played
_____play_____

8. dislike
_____like_____

9. unsafe
_____safe_____

10. cheerful
_____cheer_____

11. stamping
_____stamp_____

12. unpacked
_____pack_____

13. unfairness
_____fair_____

14. incorrectly
_____correct_____

15. replacement
_____place_____

Notes for Home: Your child identified base words. **Home Activity:** Take turns with your child writing the words 6–15 as word equations like the examples in 1–5. Use plus and equal signs.

61

Page 62

Sometimes the spelling of base words is changed when a suffix or ending is added.

The final *e* is dropped.   take   tak**ing**
The final consonant is doubled.   sit   sit**ting**
The final *y* is changed to *i*. happy   happ**iness**

Write 1, 2, or 3 to show what happened to each base word. Then write the base word.

1. The final *e* was dropped.
2. The final consonant was doubled.
3. The final *y* was changed to *i*.

1. stopped _____2_____
   stop

2. riding _____1_____
   ride

3. babies _____3_____
   baby

4. waving _____1_____
   wave

5. cutting _____2_____
   cut

6. biggest _____2_____
   big

7. stories _____3_____
   story

8. hurried _____3_____
   hurry

9. approval _____1_____
   approve

10. driver _____1_____
    drive

Notes for Home: Your child identified the changes made to the spelling of base words when suffixes or endings were added. **Home Activity:** Using the base words that were written on the lines, help your child make up an adventure story.

62

Page 63

Sometimes the spelling of a base word changes when a suffix or an ending is added.

Prefix Added
happy   **un**happy

Final *e* Dropped
drive   driver

Final Consonant Doubled
sit   sit**ting**

Final *y* Changed to *i*
baby   babies

Write the base word of each word.

1. misplace _____place_____
2. bunnies _____bunny_____
3. gladness _____glad_____
4. lovable _____love_____
5. hidden _____hid_____
6. wiggling _____wiggle_____
7. searches _____search_____
8. worried _____worry_____
9. happily _____happy_____
10. mysterious _____mystery_____

Write the base word from above that completes each sentence.

11. Our _____bunny_____ was missing.
12. How could he _____wiggle_____ out of the cage and escape?
13. We _____love_____ him very much and want to find him.
14. Our pet makes us _____happy_____.
15. When we saw he was gone, we began to cry and _____worry_____.
16. "Let's _____search_____ the yard," said Mother.
17. Our pet _____hid_____ himself very well.
18. When we found him, we were very _____glad_____.
19. We put him back in his _____place_____ in the cage.
20. The _____mystery_____ of the missing bunny was solved.

Notes for Home: Your child identified and wrote base words. **Home Activity:** Use the base words written for 1–10 to tell a story together about a family pet or adventure.

63

Page 64

The letters *ar, er, ir, or,* and *ur* stand for the vowel sounds in these words.

park   her   skirt   horn   burn

Underline 15 words in the paragraph that have a vowel-*r* sound. Then write each word under the heading where it belongs.

When the dog began to <u>bark,</u> we knew something was wrong. <u>Bert</u> and I ran to the <u>yard.</u> We saw the dog digging up <u>dirt</u> by the <u>porch.</u> A <u>large</u> turtle was stuck between two slats. We were <u>certain</u> we could be of <u>service.</u> <u>First</u> we removed some soil in a <u>circle</u> around the animal. In a <u>short</u> time, it was free. It was not <u>hurt,</u> so we <u>returned</u> it to the pond. What a great <u>story</u> we had to tell!

ar **as in** *far*
1. _____bark_____
2. _____yard_____
3. _____large_____

er **as in** *fern*
4. _____Bert_____
5. _____certain_____
6. _____service_____

ir **as in** *bird*
7. _____dirt_____
8. _____First_____
9. _____circle_____

or **as in** *fort*
10. _____porch_____
11. _____short_____
12. _____story_____

ur **as in** *turn*
13. _____turtle_____
14. _____hurt_____
15. _____returned_____

Notes for Home: Your child identified and sorted words with vowel-*r* sounds. **Home Activity:** Tell a story about a time you helped someone. Then ask your child to tell a story about a time he or she helped someone.

64

Panel 1 (page 65)

The letters *air, are, ear,* and *or* stand for the vowel sounds in these words.

chair	care	dear	word

Write the word from the box that goes with the meaning. Then circle the letters that stand for the vowel sound.

glare	clear	worst	hare	scare
near	world	pair	hear	hair

1. to frighten — sc**are**

2. what covers your head — h**air**

3. two of a kind — p**air**

4. not cloudy — cl**ear**

5. an angry look — gl**are**

6. another name for the Earth — w**or**ld

7. the opposite of *best* — w**or**st

8. close to — n**ear**

9. a kind of rabbit — h**are**

10. to listen to — h**ear**

Notes for Home: Your child matched vowel-*r* words with meaning clues.
Home Activity: Make up a sentence for a word in the box. Have your child identify the word with the vowel-*r* sound. Continue until all the words are used.

65

Panel 2 (page 66)

A suffix is added to the end of a word.

dark + ness = dark**ness**   silent + ly = silent**ly**

arm + ful = arm**ful**   humor + ous = humor**ous**

Circle the suffix that can be added to the base word to make a new word. Then write the new word.

Word	Suffixes		New Word
1. care	ly	(ful)	careful
2. great	(ness)	ous	greatness
3. final	(ly)	ous	finally
4. danger	ness	(ous)	dangerous
5. late	(ly)	ful	lately
6. joy	(ous)	ness	joyous
7. kind	(ness)	ful	kindness
8. near	(ly)	ous	nearly
9. rest	ous	(ful)	restful
10. sad	(ness)	ful	sadness
11. hope	ly	(ful)	hopeful
12. soft	ous	(ness)	softness
13. forget	ness	(ful)	forgetful
14. quick	(ly)	ous	quickly
15. vigor	(ous)	ness	vigorous

Notes for Home: Your child added suffixes to base words to make new words.
Home Activity: Have your child find words with suffixes in newspaper ads and tell what suffix was added to each word.

66

Panel 3 (page 67)

When suffixes are added to words, they change the meaning of the words.

ness = a state of being ___   dark**ness** = a state of being dark

ly = in a ___ way   loud**ly** = in a loud way

ful = full of   hope**ful** = full of hope

ous = having ___   humor**ous** = having humor

Write the word for each meaning clue. Use the underlined word and one of these suffixes: *-ness, -ly, -ful, -ous.*

1. a state of being <u>quick</u>
   quickness

2. full of <u>hope</u>
   hopeful

3. in a <u>soft</u> way
   softly

4. having <u>joy</u>
   joyous

5. full of <u>power</u>
   powerful

6. in a <u>brave</u> way
   bravely

7. having <u>danger</u>
   dangerous

8. a state of being <u>ill</u>
   illness

9. a state of being <u>sad</u>
   sadness

10. full of <u>peace</u>
    peaceful

11. in a <u>neat</u> way
    neatly

12. having <u>glamor</u>
    glamorous

13. full of <u>use</u>
    useful

14. a state of being <u>polite</u>
    politeness

15. in a <u>swift</u> way
    swiftly

Notes for Home: Your child used meaning clues and suffixes to make new words.
Home Activity: Take turns with your child using words that were written on the page to make up sentences about famous people.

67

Panel 4 (page 68)

Sometimes the spelling of a base word changes before a suffix is added.

happy − y + i + ness = happiness

Add the suffix to each base word. Write the new word.

1. merry + ly = merrily

2. mystery + ous = mysterious

3. happy + ly = happily

4. fury + ous = furious

5. crunchy + ness = crunchiness

6. victory + ous = victorious

7. empty + ness = emptiness

8. greedy + ness = greediness

9. beauty + ful = beautiful

10. melody + ous = melodious

11. easy + ly = easily

12. pretty + ness = prettiness

13. bumpy + ness = bumpiness

14. angry + ly = angrily

15. glory + ous = glorious

Notes for Home: Your child changed the spelling of base words before adding suffixes.
Home Activity: Have your child add suffixes to the words *lazy, hungry,* and *busy* and tell how the spelling had to change.

68

Answers 167

Name _____

Sometimes words have letters that do not stand for a sound.

write   **knob**   **fasten**   **gnat**   **limb**

Circle the word in each pair that has a silent consonant *w, k, t, g,* or *b.* Then write the word in the box where it belongs.

1. quarter   (knot)
2. fox   (lamb)
3. (wrench)   went
4. (listen)   hurt
5. kit   (knee)
6. germ   (design)
7. (comb)   cub
8. water   (wreath)
9. (sign)   hard
10. (glisten)   spot

silent *w*	silent *k*
11. wrench	13. knot
12. wreath	14. knee
silent *t*	silent *g*
15. listen	17. design
16. glisten	18. sign

silent *b*	
19. lamb	
20. comb	

Notes for Home: Your child identified and sorted words with silent letters.
Home Activity: Take turns with your child choosing a word, drawing a picture of it, and having the other person write the word for the picture.

69

Name _____

In some letter pairs, one letter is silent.

write   **knot**   **fasten**   **gnat**   **crumb**

Draw lines to match two words with the same silent letter. Then write each word pair and tell what letter is silent.

1. wrap — assign
2. limb — glisten
3. sign — knit
4. listen — climb
5. knee — wreath

6. comb — wreck
7. resign — knock
8. listener — lamb
9. wren — design
10. know — Christmas

11. The words __wrap__ and __wreath__ have a silent __w__.
12. The words __limb__ and __climb__ have a silent __b__.
13. The words __sign__ and __assign__ have a silent __g__.
14. The words __listen__ and __glisten__ have a silent __t__.
15. The words __knee__ and __knit__ have a silent __k__.
16. The words __comb__ and __lamb__ have a silent __b__.
17. The words __resign__ and __design__ have a silent __g__.
18. The words __listener__ and __Christmas__ have a silent __t__.
19. The words __wren__ and __wreck__ have a silent __w__.
20. The words __know__ and __knock__ have a silent __k__.

Notes for Home: Your child identified silent letters in words. **Home Activity:** Take turns with your child making up a silly sentence for each pair of words and telling what letter is silent in the two words.

70

Name _____

The letters *th, ch, ph,* and *sh* can sometimes be found in the middle of words. The two letters stand for one sound.

father   **reached**   **telephone**   **bookshelf**

Circle the letters that stand for the sound you hear in the middle of each picture name.

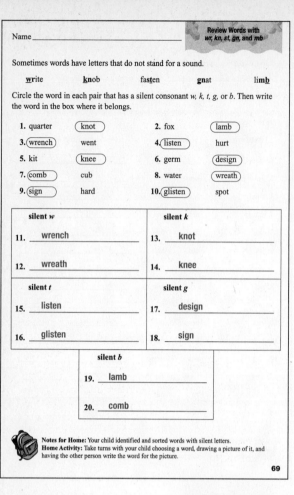

1.   (th)   ch   ph   sh
2.   th   ch   (ph)   sh
3.   th   (ch)   ph   sh
4.   th   ch   ph   (sh)
5.   (th)   ch   ph   sh
6.   th   ch   (ch)   ph   sh
7.   th   ch   ph   (sh)
8.   th   ch   ph   (sh)
9.   th   ch   (ph)   sh
10.   (th)   ch   ph   sh

Notes for Home: Your child identified consonant digraphs in the middle of words.
Home Activity: Have your child choose one of these consonant digraphs: *th, ch, ph, sh.* Together write all the words you can think of with these letters in the middle.

71

Name _____

The letters *th, ch, ph,* and *sh* can sometimes be found in the middle of words.

gather   **reaches**   **telephone**   **fishing**

Write the word from the box that answers each clue. Circle the letters *th, ch, ph,* or *sh* that appear in the middle of the word.

peaches	alphabet	trophy	seashells	perches
weather	elephant	beaches	father	bookshelves

1. This animal has a trunk.   ele(ph)ant
2. A dad may be called this.   fa(th)er
3. A beach is where these can be found.   sea(sh)ells
4. Rain, snow, and sun are part of this.   wea(th)er
5. You might win this as a prize.   tro(ph)y
6. A library has many of these for books.   book(sh)elves
7. These feel fuzzy to the touch.   pea(ch)es
8. These are sandy places.   bea(ch)es
9. This is another name for the ABC's.   al(ph)abet
10. These are places for birds to rest.   per(ch)es

Notes for Home: Your child wrote words with consonant digraphs in the middle.
Home Activity: Choose a word from the box and make up a clue for it. Ask your child to guess the word. Then have your child choose a word.

72

Sometimes the letters *th*, *ch*, *ph*, and *sh* stand for sounds heard in the middle of words.

| anything | reaches | telephone | dashed |

Write *th*, *ch*, *ph*, or *sh* to complete a word that makes sense in the sentence.

1. Look at that big gray ele_p_ _h_ant.

2. I hope we have sun_s_ _h_ine and not rain today.

3. Fill the ba_t_ _h_tub with warm water.

4. Who coa_c_ _h_es your team?

5. My grandfa_t_ _h_er is coming for a visit.

6. Consuelo collects sea_s_ _h_ells.

7. Did you buy any_t_ _h_ing at the store?

8. My grades are un_c_ _h_anged.

9. The first-prize winner received a tro_p_ _h_y.

10. Do you know the al_p_ _h_abet song?

11. A crowd ga_t_ _h_ered to watch the parade.

12. I like poa_c_ _h_ed eggs.

13. Please re_c_ _h_eck your work.

14. A go_p_ _h_er dug tunnels under our lawn.

15. Your friend_s_ _h_ip is important to me.

Notes for Home: Your child wrote consonant digraphs in the middle of words.
Home Activity: Take turns with your child writing other words with the letters *th*, *ch*, *ph*, or *sh* in the middle, leaving out the letters, and having the other person write the missing letters.

73

A base word is a word without any prefixes, suffixes, or endings added.

| | rerun | neighborhood | singing |
| Base Words: | run | neighbor | sing |

Add the prefixes, suffixes, or endings shown to the base word to make new words.

lock

1. un + _lock_ = _unlock_

2. _lock_ + ing = _locking_

3. _lock_ + er = _locker_

play

4. re + _play_ = _replay_

5. _play_ + ed = _played_

6. _play_ + er = _player_

correct

7. in + _correct_ = _incorrect_

8. _correct_ + ing = _correcting_

9. _correct_ + ion = _correction_

10. in + _correct_ + ly = _incorrectly_

Notes for Home: Your child added prefixes, suffixes, and endings to base words.
Home Activity: Take turns with your child choosing a base word, adding a prefix, suffix, or ending, and then using the new word in a sentence.

74

When suffixes or endings are added to base words, the spelling of the base word sometimes changes.

Drop the final *e*.	come = coming
Double the final consonant.	run = running
Change *y* to *i*.	try = tries
No change	sing = singing

Write each word in the box that shows how the base word was changed.

armful	mysterious	lovable	biggest	worried
location	nearly	librarian	dirtiest	determination
approval	searches	hesitated	hidden	neighborhood
shutting	careful	memories	swimming	beginner

Drop the Final *e*	Double the Final Consonant
1. _location_	6. _shutting_
2. _approval_	7. _biggest_
3. _lovable_	8. _hidden_
4. _hesitated_	9. _swimming_
5. _determination_	10. _beginner_

Change *y* to *i*	No Change
11. _mysterious_	16. _armful_
12. _librarian_	17. _nearly_
13. _memories_	18. _searches_
14. _dirtiest_	19. _careful_
15. _worried_	20. _neighborhood_

Notes for Home: Your child identified the spelling changes made to base words when suffixes or endings are added. **Home Activity:** Have your child add one more word to each list.

75

Consonants blends, such as *bl*, *gl*, and *st*, can stand for the beginning sound in a word.

Circle the blend that stands for the sound at the beginning of each picture name. Then write the blend to complete the word.

1. (st) sp
_s_ _t_ ar

2. (gr) gl
_g_ _r_ apes

3. pr (pl)
_p_ _l_ ane

4. (fl) fr
_f_ _l_ ower

5. (dr) tr
_d_ _r_ ill

6. fl (fr)
_f_ _r_ uit

7. (sp) st
_s_ _p_ ool

8. (sm) sn
_s_ _m_ ile

9. (bl) br
_b_ _l_ ock

10. gr (gl)
_g_ _l_ asses

Notes for Home: Your child identified initial consonant blends in words.
Home Activity: Choose a consonant blend from the page and name two words that begin with the blend. Then have your child choose a blend and name two words for it.

76

Answers **169**

Page 77

Name_____ **Consonant Blends**

Consonant blends, such as *st, nt,* and *mp,* can stand for the ending sound in a word.

Circle the picture whose name has the ending sound spelled by the consonant blend.

1. nt *(tent circled)*
2. mp *(lamp circled)*
3. st *(nest circled)*
4. st *(vest circled)*
5. nd *(hand circled)*
6. lt *(belt circled)*
7. mp *(stamp circled)*
8. sk *(desk circled)*
9. nt *(plant circled)*
10. ld *(shield circled)*

Notes for Home: Your child identified the final consonant blends in words.
Home Activity: Name a word that ends with a consonant blend. Write the letters that stand for the ending sound. Then ask your child to do the same.

77

Page 78

Name_____ **Consonant Blends**

Consonant blends can stand for the sound at the beginning of words.
Consonant blends can stand for the sound at the end of words.

Fill in the circle under the blend that begins or ends each picture name.

Beginning

1. fr · **br** · tr
2. sn · **st** · sp
3. tr · **gl** · pr
4. **sl** · sm · st
5. bl · pl · **fl**

Ending

6. mp · nd · **nt**
7. **lt** · nd · ld
8. ct · lt · **nt**
9. **st** · nt · lt
10. st · **sk** · nd

Notes for Home: Your child identified initial or final consonant blends in picture names.
Home Activity: With your child, look through a newspaper. Circle words with beginning or ending blends.

78

Page 79

Name_____ **Review Digraphs**
th, ch, ph, and *sh*

Consonant digraphs, such as *th, ch, ph,* and *sh,* sometimes come in the middle of words. The two letters stand for one sound.

   another   reaching   go**ph**er   finished

Write the word from the list that completes each sentence. Circle the digraph that is found in the middle of the word.

inchworm	father	telephone	feather	trophy
branches	washing	elephant	seashells	bookshelves
teacher	weather	bathtub	mushrooms	alphabet

1. Circus goes with ___elephant___ . th ch **ph** sh
2. Prize goes with ___trophy___ . th ch **ph** sh
3. Moth goes with ___inchworm___ . th **ch** ph sh
4. Mother goes with ___father___ . **th** ch ph sh
5. School goes with ___teacher___ . th **ch** ph sh
6. Beach goes with ___seashells___ . th ch ph **sh**
7. Tree goes with ___branches___ . th **ch** ph sh
8. Library goes with ___bookshelves___ . th ch ph **sh**
9. Rain goes with ___weather___ . **th** ch ph sh
10. ABC goes with ___alphabet___ . th ch **ph** sh
11. Cleaning goes with ___washing___ . th ch ph **sh**
12. Shower goes with ___bathtub___ . **th** ch ph sh
13. Call goes with ___telephone___ . th ch **ph** sh
14. Bird goes with ___feather___ . **th** ch ph sh
15. Pizza goes with ___mushrooms___ . th ch ph **sh**

Notes for Home: Your child identified consonant digraphs in the middle of words.
Home Activity: Go through the sentences together. Take turns giving another word that could complete each sentence.

79

Page 80

Name_____ **Review Digraphs**
th, ch, ph, and *sh*

Father, inchworm, elephant, and *fishing* all have consonant digraphs in the middle.

Circle the word in each question that has a *th, ch, ph,* or *sh* in the middle. Then use the circled word to write an answer to the question.
                         Answers to questions will vary.

1. Where might you see an (elephant)?
   You might see an elephant at a zoo.

2. What does a (flashlight) need to work?
   A flashlight needs batteries to work.

3. Where do you put (toothpaste)?
   You put toothpaste on a toothbrush.

4. What game do you play with your (brother)?
   You might play chess with your brother.

5. Where could you find a (seashell)?
   You could find a seashell on a beach.

6. What does a (teacher) do?
   A teacher teaches students many subjects.

7. Who might win a (trophy)?
   A person who wins a race might get a trophy.

8. How do (peaches) taste?
   Peaches taste juicy and sweet.

9. What is the last letter of the (alphabet)?
   The last letter of the alphabet is *z.*

10. What could you make in a (workshop)?
    You could make a table in a workshop.

Notes for Home: Your child identified words with medial consonant digraphs.
Home Activity: Choose a circled word from the page and ask a question, using the word in the question. Have your child answer the question.

80

170 Answers

Some consonant blends, such as *scr, str,* and *spr,* have three letters. They can stand for the beginning sound in a word.

Circle the letters that stand for the beginning sound in the picture name. Add the circled letters to the letters shown to make a new word.

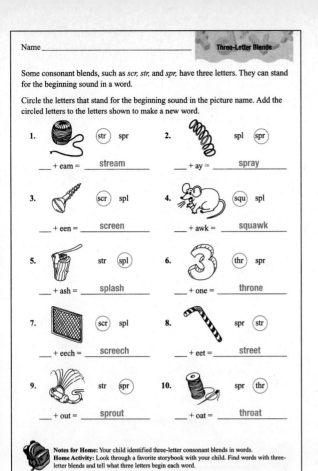

1. (str) spr
___ + eam = **stream**

2. spl (spr)
___ + ay = **spray**

3. (scr) spl
___ + een = **screen**

4. (squ) spl
___ + awk = **squawk**

5. str (spl)
___ + ash = **splash**

6. (thr) spr
___ + one = **throne**

7. (scr) spl
___ + eech = **screech**

8. spr (str)
___ + eet = **street**

9. str (spr)
___ + out = **sprout**

10. spr (thr)
___ + oat = **throat**

Notes for Home: Your child identified three-letter consonant blends in words.
Home Activity: Look through a favorite storybook with your child. Find words with three-letter blends and tell what three letters begin each word.

81

Consonant blends with three letters, such as *spr, spl,* or *thr,* can come at the beginning of a word. The three letters stand for one sound.

Make new words. Change the underlined letter or letters in each word. Add the three-letter blend. Write the new word.

scr
1. <u>b</u>eam   **scream**
2. <u>b</u>een   **screen**

squ
3. <u>sp</u>eak   **squeak**
4. <u>s</u>neeze   **squeeze**

spl
5. <u>w</u>inter   **splinter**
6. <u>c</u>rash   **splash**

spr
7. <u>f</u>ling   **spring**
8. <u>tw</u>inkle   **sprinkle**

str
9. <u>sw</u>eet   **street**
10. <u>ch</u>ange   **strange**

thr
11. <u>m</u>ust   **thrust**
12. <u>c</u>oat   **throat**

Complete each sentence. Use a word you wrote above.

13. When I am scared, I **scream** .
14. A mouse might make a **squeak** .
15. The season before summer is **spring** .
16. I have a sore **throat** .
17. In a swimming pool, people like to **splash** .
18. Look both ways when crossing a **street** .
19. A hug is a big **squeeze** .
20. A window might be covered by a **screen** .

Notes for Home: Your child wrote words with three-letter blends. Home Activity: Take turns with your child pointing to a three-letter blend and naming a word that begins with that blend.

82

Three-letter blends stand for the beginning sounds in these words.

squeak   **str**eet   **thr**ee

Write the word that answers the question. Circle the blend.

1. Does a mouse **scream** or **squeak**?   (squ)eak
2. Is **spring** or **string** a season?   (spr)ing
3. Would you **sprig** or **splash** in a bathtub?   (spl)ash
4. Are eggs usually **scrambled** or **scraped**?   (scr)ambled
5. Does a **screw** or a **scrap** hold something together?   (scr)ew
6. Would a shirt have **stripes** or **scrunches**?   (str)ipes
7. Does a backpack have a **strap** or a **sprain**?   (str)ap
8. Is a **square** or a **scream** a shape?   (squ)are
9. Do you **split** or **strain** wood?   (spl)it
10. Does a **splinter** or a **sprinkler** water a lawn?   (spr)inkler
11. Is **three** or **through** an age?   (thr)ee
12. Might a cat **squeeze** or **scratch** you?   (scr)atch
13. Could a **throat** or a **throne** feel sore?   (thr)oat
14. Might you **sprout** or **sprain** an ankle?   (spr)ain
15. Would you **scrub** or **scratch** a floor to make it clean?   (scr)ub

Notes for Home: Your child identified words with three-letter blends.
Home Activity: Have your child use each word he or she wrote in a sentence.

83

A consonant blend can stand for the sound at the beginning or end of a word.

drum   **cl**oud   **sm**all
hand   **ask**   **cold**

Write each word in the box where it belongs. Then write the blend or blends found in the words.

mask	meant	gleam	gold	friend
train	lamp	bend	plate	vest
guest	dry	smile	risk	spider
greed	crust	scout	belt	steam

Beginning Blends		Ending Blends	
1. train — tr		10. mask — sk	
2. greed — gr		11. guest — st	
3. dry — dr		12. meant — nt	
4. gleam — gl		13. lamp — mp	
5. smile — sm		14. bend — nd	
6. scout — sc		15. gold — ld	
7. plate — pl		16. risk — sk	
8. spider — sp		17. belt — lt	
9. steam — st		18. vest — st	

Both Beginning and Ending Blends		
19. crust — cr — st		
20. friend — fr — nd		

Notes for Home: Your child wrote words with initial and final consonant blends.
Home Activity: Ask your child to choose a word from the page and to name another word with the same beginning or ending blend. Then you take a turn.

84

Answers **171**

A consonant blend can stand for the sound at the beginning or end of a word.

drum   grapes   plate   hand   mask   stamp

Circle the blend in each word. Then write the words where they belong in the sentence. Some words will not be used.

(sn)ow   me(lt)   sa(nd)

1. The _____snow_____ began to _____melt_____ in the sun.

to(st)   (gr)apes   (sk)ates

2. We ate juicy _____grapes_____ and crunchy _____toast_____.

be(lt)   ne(st)   (dr)ess

3. Mom bought a _____belt_____ and a _____dress_____.

la(mp)   (pl)ane   c(l)oud

4. I saw a _____plane_____ and a _____cloud_____ in the sky.

(sw)eep   (br)oom   (sp)oon

5. Get a _____broom_____ and _____sweep_____ the floor.

Notes for Home: Your child wrote words with initial and final consonant blends.
Home Activity: Have your child choose three words from the page and use any two of the words to make a new sentence.

85

The letters *oi* and *oy* stand for the vowel sound in these words.

coin   boy

Write the word that completes each phrase. Circle the letters that stand for the vowel sound.

joy	noise	choice	enjoy	join
point	royal	cowboy	toy	voyage
soil	loyal	oil	voice	annoying

1. a _____toy_____ to play with   oi   (oy)
2. full of happiness and _____joy_____   oi   (oy)
3. need _____oil_____ for the squeak   (oi)   oy
4. to _____join_____ the two ends   (oi)   oy
5. seeds growing in _____soil_____   (oi)   oy
6. a loud _____noise_____   (oi)   oy
7. the _____royal_____ prince and princess   oi   (oy)
8. her beautiful singing _____voice_____   (oi)   oy
9. a broken pencil _____point_____   (oi)   oy
10. that _____cowboy_____ rounding up cattle   oi   (oy)
11. an _____annoying_____ buzzing sound   oi   (oy)
12. a _____choice_____ between two things   (oi)   oy
13. a _____voyage_____ across the ocean   oi   (oy)
14. to _____enjoy_____ the movie   oi   (oy)
15. a _____loyal_____ fan of the football team   oi   (oy)

Notes for Home: Your child wrote words with the vowel diphthongs *oi* and *oy*.
Home Activity: Take turns with your child using the phrases on the page to make sentences. Then pick one sentence and use it to begin a story that you make up together.

86

The letters *oi* and *oy* stand for the vowel sound in *soil* and *boy*.

Write the word from the list that rhymes with the word in the box. Circle the letters that stand for the vowel sound. Then follow the directions.

enjoy   disappoint   royal   coin   voice

1. | join | _____coin_____   (oi)   oy

Add *-ed* to the end of each word.

_____joined_____   _____coined_____

2. | loyal | _____royal_____   oi   (oy)

Add *-ty* to the end of each word.

_____loyalty_____   _____royalty_____

3. | employ | _____enjoy_____   oi   (oy)

Add *-ment* to the end of each word.

_____employment_____   _____enjoyment_____

4. | anoint | _____disappoint_____   (oi)   oy

Add *-ing* to the end of each word.

_____anointing_____   _____disappointing_____

5. | rejoice | _____voice_____   (oi)   oy

Take off the final *e* and add *-ing* to each word.

_____rejoicing_____   _____voicing_____

Notes for Home: Your child wrote words with the vowel diphthongs *oi* and *oy*.
Home Activity: Together list other words that have *oi* or *oy* in them. Take turns with your child naming words that rhyme with the words in the list.

87

Oil and *joy* have the same vowel sound. The letters *oi* and *oy* stand for that vowel sound.

Write a word from the list next to the word that is almost alike in meaning. Circle the letters that stand for the vowel sound you hear in *oil*.

| loyal | toy | toil | oyster |
| joyful | spoil | join | voyage |

1. happy   _____j(oy)ful_____   2. rot   _____sp(oi)l_____
3. faithful _____l(oy)al_____   4. plaything _____t(oy)_____
5. connect   _____j(oi)n_____   6. work   _____t(oi)l_____
7. shellfish _____(oy)ster_____   8. trip   _____v(oy)age_____

Write a word from the list next to the word that is opposite in meaning. Circle the letters that stand for the vowel sound you hear in *oil*.

| destroy | moist | loyal | noisy |
| boy | unemployed | joy | |

9. sadness   _____j(oy)_____   10. girl   _____b(oy)_____
11. dry   _____m(oi)st_____   12. build   _____destr(oy)_____
13. quiet   _____n(oi)sy_____   14. employed _____unempl(oy)ed_____
15. disloyal _____l(oy)al_____

Notes for Home: Your child wrote words with the vowel diphthongs *oi* and *oy*.
Home Activity: Have your child look through newspaper and magazine ads for words with *oi* and *oy*. Read the words together.

88

---

172 Answers

A consonant blend with three letters, such as *str*, *spl*, or *thr*, stands for one sound.

string   **spl**ash   **thr**ee

Use the clues to complete the puzzle.

thread   sprinkler   square   strikes   strawberry
scream   scrub   three   streets   splash

Across

1. used to water a lawn
2. in baseball, three and you are out
5. to wash something by rubbing it hard
6. a red fruit
8. a shape with four equal sides

Down

1. places where cars drive
3. use a needle to sew with this
4. a loud, high yell
5. something people do in a swimming pool
7. the number between two and four

	¹S	P	R	I	N	K	L	E	R		²S	T	³R	I	K	E	⁴S
	T												H				C
⁵S	C	R	U	B		⁶S	⁷T	R	A	W	B	E	R	R	Y		R
P	E					H						E					E
L	E					R						A					A
A	T					E						D					M
S			⁸S	Q	U	A	R	E									
H																	

Notes for Home: Your child completed a puzzle, using words with three-letter blends. **Home Activity:** Have your child choose one of these blends: *scr, spl, str, squ, spr, thr.* Together write as many words as you can that begin with the blend.

89

A consonant blend may have three letters that stand for one sound.

scream   **squ**are   **thr**ee

Write each word in the box that has the same three-letter blend.

strong   spring   splash   string   squeak
thrill   throw   stream   squirrel   spray
splinter   square   spread   thread   straw
scratch   split   scream   scrub   three

scr	spl
1. scratch	4. splinter
2. scream	5. split
3. scrub	6. splash

spr	squ
7. spring	10. square
8. spread	11. squirrel
9. spray	12. squeak

str	thr
13. strong	17. thrill
14. stream	18. throw
15. string	19. thread
16. straw	20. three

Notes for Home: Your child sorted words with three-letter blends. **Home Activity:** Take turns with your child choosing any three words from the list at the top of the page and putting the words in alphabetical order.

90

A possessive shows that something belongs to someone or something.

- Add *'s* to make a singular noun possessive.   doctor   doctor**'s**
- Add *'s* to make a plural noun possessive.   men   men**'s**
- Add *'* to a plural noun that ends in *s*.   twins   twins**'**

Make each singular or plural noun possessive.

1. girl   girl's
2. boy   boy's
3. Maria   Maria's
4. Lee   Lee's
5. children children's
6. family   family's
7. book   book's
8. tiger   tiger's
9. herd   herd's
10. flock   flock's

Make each plural noun possessive.

11. dogs   dogs'
12. teachers teachers'
13. shells   shells'
14. girls   girls'
15. mice   mice's
16. geese   geese's
17. bunnies   bunnies'
18. women   women's
19. foxes   foxes'
20. cities   cities'

Notes for Home: Your child wrote possessive forms of singular and plural nouns. **Home Activity:** Point to an object. Ask your child to name the object, write its name, say the possessive, and then write it. Example: *book, book's.*

91

A possessive shows that something belongs to someone or something.

- Add *'s* to make a singular noun possessive.   cat   cat**'s**
- Add *'s* to make a plural noun possessive.   mice   mice**'s**
- Add *'* to a plural noun that ends in *s*.   dogs   dogs**'**

Change each phrase into a phrase with a possessive.

Example: the stripes of the tiger = the tiger's stripes

1. the tractor that belongs to the farmer   the farmer's tractor
2. a pool for the penguins   the penguins' pool
3. a pencil that Keesha owns   Keesha's pencil
4. that game that the twins own   the twins' game
5. some seed for the parrots   the parrots' seed
6. the book belonging to Juan   Juan's book
7. this car belonging to that family   that family's car
8. a ball that the cat has   the cat's ball
9. the flowers belonging to those people   those people's flowers
10. the chains for the necklaces   the necklaces' chains
11. a bike for Kwan   Kwan's bike
12. the park belonging to the community   the community's park
13. some cages for the lions   the lions' cages
14. some shoes belonging to the children   the children's shoes
15. this report belonging to the group   the group's report

Notes for Home: Your child wrote phrases with possessives. **Home Activity:** Take turns with your child writing possessive phrases, such as *Mary's book* or *the dogs' bones.*

92

Answers **173**

Here is how to make nouns possessive:

singular noun	sister	sister**'s**
plural noun	women	women**'s**
plural noun ending in *s*	brothers	brothers**'**

Write the possessive noun in each phrase. After each noun, write **S** for singular noun or **P** for plural noun.

1. doctor's office
   doctor's _____ S

2. children's games
   children's _____ P

3. sisters' friend
   sisters' _____ P

4. lion's paw
   lion's _____ S

5. men's hats
   men's _____ P

6. woman's picture
   woman's _____ S

Rewrite each sentence. Use the possessive form of the noun in parentheses.

7. We had a party for my ___ anniversary. (parents)
   We had a party for my parents' anniversary.

8. My ___ family came from Tampa. (mother)
   My mother's family came from Tampa.

9. ___ brother flew in from Dallas. (Dad)
   Dad's brother flew in from Dallas.

10. Our ___ celebration was a big success. (family)
    Our family's celebration was a big success.

Notes for Home: Your child identified and wrote possessive nouns.
Home Activity: Have your child look through a favorite book for examples of possessives and tell who owns what.

93

The letters *oi* and *oy* stand for the vowel sound in *join* and *toy*.

Read each sentence. Write one or two words that have the same vowel sound as *join* and *toy*.

The boys made a lot of noise playing in the yard.

1. boys

2. noise

First, boil the potatoes, and then wrap them in foil.

3. boil

4. foil

Try to join these two coils of rope.

5. join

6. coils

The cowboy had a loud singing voice.

7. cowboy

8. voice

The loyal worker was a good employee.

9. loyal

10. employee

An oyster tastes good dipped in soy sauce.

11. oyster

12. soy

The family enjoyed the sea voyage.

13. enjoyed

14. voyage

Use oil to fix the door hinge.

15. oil

Notes for Home: Your child identified and wrote words with *oi* and *oy*.
Home Activity: Have your child choose two words he or she wrote on the page and make up a new sentence using the words.

94

The letters *oi* and *oy* stand for the vowel sound in *join* and *toy*.

Circle 12 hidden words with *oi* and *oy*. Write the words you circle.
Hint: Two words are small words within bigger words.

```
t  o  y  b  c  m  o  i  s  t  p  o  i  n  t
d  e  f  g  s  p  o  i  l  n  o  i  s  e  h
k  l  b  o  y  m  p  r  s  j  o  y  f  u  l
l  o  y  a  l  s  v  o  i  c  e  g  d  n  s
r  h  v  o  y  a  g  e  b  f  h  m  k  r  s
```

1. toy

2. moist

3. point

4. spoil

5. oil

6. noise

7. boy

8. joyful

9. joy

10. loyal

11. voice

12. voyage

Write the word from above that means the same as the phrase.

13. a plaything — toy

14. the tip of a pencil — point

15. very happy — joyful

Notes for Home: Your child wrote words with *oi* and *oy*. **Home Activity:** Together make a word-search puzzle like the one on the page. Use words with *oi* and *oy*.

95

The letters *ar, er, ir, or,* and *ur* stand for the vowel sounds in these words.

card	her	third	born	turn

Write the word that answers each question. Then write the letters that stand for the vowel-*r* sound in the word.

1. Do you eat with a fort or a fork? — fork — or

2. Would you sir or stir pancake batter? — stir — ir

3. Might you sit on a front port or porch? — porch — or

4. Does a rabbit have fur or spurs? — fur — ur

5. Could you see a star or a start in the sky? — star — ar

6. Do you drink water because you are thirsty or thirty? — thirsty — ir

7. Is a gift for or forth someone? — for — or

8. Would you turn or burn a candle for light? — burn — ur

9. Do ferns or terms grow in the woods? — ferns — er

10. Does a shirt or a skirt have sleeves? — shirt — ir

Notes for Home: Your child wrote vowel-*r* words and identified vowel-*r* spellings.
Home Activity: With your child, look through newspapers. Have your child use a crayon to circle words with *ar, er, ir, or,* and *ur*.

96

---

174 Answers

Name _____

The letters *ar, er, ir, or,* and *ur* stand for the vowel sounds in these words.

start	her	first	for	turn

Write the word from the box that rhymes with each picture name. Then write the letters that stand for the vowel-*r* sound.

cork	stern	third	fur	dirt
jar	thorn	nurse	farm	bark

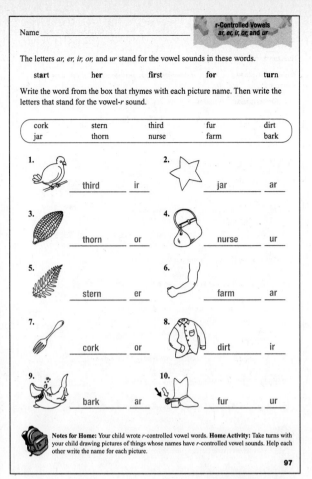

1. third — ir
2. jar — ar
3. thorn — or
4. nurse — ur
5. stern — er
6. farm — ar
7. cork — or
8. dirt — ir
9. bark — ar
10. fur — ur

Notes for Home: Your child wrote *r*-controlled vowel words. **Home Activity:** Take turns with your child drawing pictures of things whose names have *r*-controlled vowel sounds. Help each other write the name for each picture.

97

Name _____

The letters *ear* and *our* stand for the vowel sounds in these words

learn	four

Write each word under the word that has the same vowel-*r* sound. Some words will not be written.

early	pour	court	our	fear
clear	source	heard	course	earth
earn	hour	mourn	search	hear

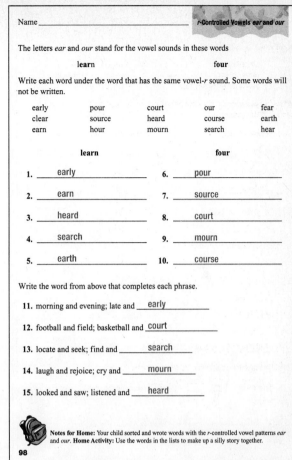

learn	**four**
1. early	6. pour
2. earn	7. source
3. heard	8. court
4. search	9. mourn
5. earth	10. course

Write the word from above that completes each phrase.

11. morning and evening; late and __early__

12. football and field; basketball and __court__

13. locate and seek; find and __search__

14. laugh and rejoice; cry and __mourn__

15. looked and saw; listened and __heard__

Notes for Home: Your child sorted and wrote words with the *r*-controlled vowel patterns *ear* and *our*. **Home Activity:** Use the words in the lists to make up a silly story together.

98

Name _____

Suffixes are added to the ends of words.

kind**ness**	bright**ly**	help**ful**	humor**ous**

Use a word from the box to complete each tongue twister. Then write the suffix that appears at the end of the word.

sadly	finally	powerful	delightful	poisonous
glamorous	greatness	lively	illness	wonderful

1. Leo Lion likes __lively__ leaps. — ly

2. Wendy's __wonderful__ wagon won. — ful

3. Greta's __greatness__ grew gradually. — ness

4. Firefighters __finally__ found frisky Fluffy. — ly

5. Sarah sat __sadly__ on the soft, silky sofa. — ly

6. Dora dug __delightful__, dainty daffodils. — ful

7. Inez's __illness__ is itchy and infectious. — ness

8. Please pull perilous, pesky, __poisonous__ plants. — ous

9. Gloria's glimmering, __glamorous__ gloves glittered. — ous

10. Pretty, __powerful__ ponies pulled the plows. — ful

Notes for Home: Your child wrote words with suffixes. **Home Activity:** Take turns with your child saying tongue twisters you know. Then make up some tongue twisters that have words with suffixes.

99

Name _____

Sometimes when a suffix is added to the end of a word, a spelling change is needed. Sometimes no spelling change is needed.

No spelling change is needed.   kind + ness = kindness
If a word ends in *y*, the *y* is changed to *i*.   beauty – y + i + ful = beautiful

Underline the answer to the question. Write the new word.

1. **bright**
Does the word end in *y*? Yes (No)
Add **ly**. Write the word.
brightiy

2. **happy**
Does the word end in *y*? (Yes) No
Add **ness**. Write the word.
happiness

3. **angry**
Does the word end in *y*? (Yes) No
Add **ly**. Write the word.
angrily

4. **marvel**
Does the word end in *y*? Yes (No)
Add **ous**. Write the word.
marvelous

5. **humor**
Does the word end in *y*? Yes (No)
Add **ous**. Write the word.
humorous

6. **fury**
Does the word end in *y*? (Yes) No
Add **ous**. Write the word.
furious

7. **danger**
Does the word end in *y*? Yes (No)
Add **ous**. Write the word.
dangerous

8. **empty**
Does the word end in *y*? (Yes) No
Add **ness**. Write the word.
emptiness

9. **easy**
Does the word end in *y*? (Yes) No
Add **ly**. Write the word.
easily

10. **power**
Does the word end in *y*? Yes (No)
Add **ful**. Write the word.
powerful

Notes for Home: Your child added suffixes to words, making spelling changes if necessary. **Home Activity:** Have your child make up a sentence for each word he or she wrote on the page.

100

Answers **175**

Nouns that name more than one person, place, or thing are called plural nouns.

- Add -s to most nouns to make them plural.   dog   dogs
- Add -es to nouns that end in s, ss, x, ch, and sh.   lunch   lunches

Write the plural of each noun.

1. plane   planes
2. pilot   pilots
3. field   fields
4. box   boxes
5. wish   wishes
6. paper   papers
7. glass   glasses
8. shed   sheds
9. brush   brushes
10. beach   beaches
11. week   weeks
12. push   pushes
13. pass   passes
14. friend   friends
15. circus   circuses

Use words you wrote above to complete the sentences.

16. The _pilots_ landed the plane safely.

17. Corn is growing in those _fields_.

18. How many _weeks_ are in a year?

19. He drank two _glasses_ of milk.

20. How many _boxes_ of cereal are on the shelf?

Notes for Home: Your child formed the plurals of words by adding s or es.
Home Activity: Take turns with your child pointing to an object, saying the plural form of its name, and writing the plural form.

If a word ends in a vowel and y, -s is added to make the word mean more than one.

monkey + s = monkeys

If a word ends in a consonant and y, the y is changed to i, and -es is added to make the word mean more than one.

baby – y + i + es = babies

Underline *vowel* or *consonant* to answer the question. Then add -s or -es and write the plural form of the word.

Word	Question	Plural
1. day	Is the letter before y a <u>vowel</u> or a consonant?	days
2. toy	Is the letter before y a <u>vowel</u> or a consonant?	toys
3. puppy	Is the letter before y a vowel or a <u>consonant</u>?	puppies
4. key	Is the letter before y a <u>vowel</u> or a consonant?	keys
5. berry	Is the letter before y a vowel or a <u>consonant</u>?	berries
6. boy	Is the letter before y a <u>vowel</u> or a consonant?	boys
7. bunny	Is the letter before y a vowel or a <u>consonant</u>?	bunnies
8. city	Is the letter before y a vowel or a <u>consonant</u>?	cities
9. body	Is the letter before y a vowel or a <u>consonant</u>?	bodies
10. delay	Is the letter before y a <u>vowel</u> or a consonant?	delays

Notes for Home: Your child wrote the plural forms of words ending in y.
Home Activity: With your child, look for nouns that end in y. Tell how to make the plural. Use the question on the page to help decide whether to make a spelling change.

Some nouns make their plurals in unusual ways.

1. If the noun ends in f or fe, the f or fe is changed to v, and -es is added.   shelf   shelves
2. Some nouns use a new word.   man   men
3. Some nouns use the same word.   deer   deer

Write 1, 2, or 3 to tell how each plural was formed. Use the numbered list above.

1. mouse/mice   2
2. sheep/sheep   3
3. wolf/wolves   1
4. woman/women   2
5. child/children   2
6. foot/feet   2
7. knife/knives   1
8. leaf/leaves   1
9. calf/calves   1
10. goose/geese   2

Write 1, 2, or 3 to show how to make each word plural. Then write the new word.

11. wife   1   wives
12. tooth   2   teeth
13. moose   3   moose
14. loaf   1   loaves
15. gentleman   2   gentlemen

Notes for Home: Your child wrote the plural forms of nouns whose plurals are formed in unusual ways. Home Activity: Have your child look in newspapers for plural nouns and tell how each plural was formed. Use the numbered list on the page for help.

Remember how possessive nouns are made:

- For a singular noun, add 's.   aunt   aunt's
- For a plural noun, add 's.   men   men's
- For a plural noun that ends in s, add '.   uncles   uncles'

Write the possessive of the word in parentheses to complete each phrase.

1. (pony)   the _pony's_ mane
2. (schools)   the _schools'_ flags
3. (Smith)   Mrs. _Smith's_ house
4. (children)   the _children's_ books
5. (girls)   the _girls'_ shoes
6. (workers)   the _workers'_ tools
7. (men)   the _men's_ races
8. (fox)   the _fox's_ tail
9. (sheep)   the _sheep's_ wool
10. (women)   the _women's_ hats

Notes for Home: Your child wrote singular and plural possessive nouns.
Home Activity: Have your child name a person and something he or she might own and then write the name and the object in a possessive phrase. Example: Mary book, Mary's book.

Panel 1 (page 105)

Name_____   **Review Possessives**

A possessive shows that something belongs to someone or something.

- Add 's to make a singular noun possessive.   neighbor   neighbor's
- Add 's to make a plural noun possessive.   people   people's
- Add ' to a plural noun that ends in s.   planes   planes'

Write the possessive form of each noun. Then add a word to show something that is owned.
Answers will vary.

Example: swan   swan's   swan's feathers

1. boy	boy's	boy's face
2. cats	cats'	cats' whiskers
3. men	men's	men's jackets
4. mothers	mothers'	mothers' stories
5. bird	bird's	bird's beak
6. children	children's	children's books
7. turtles	turtles'	turtles' shells
8. teachers	teachers'	teachers' lounge
9. chair	chair's	chair's seat
10. sister	sister's	sister's room
11. women	women's	women's shoes
12. tree	tree's	tree's branches
13. sheep	sheep's	sheep's wool
14. insects	insects'	insects' wings
15. mice	mice's	mice's feet

Notes for Home: Your child wrote possessive nouns and possessive phrases.
Home Activity: Take turns with your child using the possessive phrases he or she wrote to create oral sentences. Tell which word is the possessive and whether it is singular or plural.

105

Panel 2 (page 106)

Name_____   **Consonant /k/: c, ck, ch**

The *k* sound can be spelled by the letters *c, ck,* or *ch.*

color   neck   chord

Sort the words to show what letter or letters stand for /k/ in each word.

back	ache	can	stomach	careful
thick	because	cut	vacation	coat
anchor	traffic	echo	track	wreck
bucket	fact	clock	count	recall

/k/ = c

1. because		2. traffic
3. fact		4. can
5. cut		6. vacation
7. count		8. careful
9. coat		10. recall

/k/ = ck

11. back		12. thick
13. bucket		14. clock
15. track		16. wreck

/k/ = ch

17. anchor		18. ache
19. echo		20. stomach

Notes for Home: Your child wrote words with /k/ spelled *c, ck,* or *ch.*
Home Activity: With your child, look through the Yellow Pages in a telephone book for words with /k/ spelled *c, ck,* or *ch.*

106

Panel 3 (page 107)

Name_____   **Consonant /k/: c, ck, ch**

The letters *c, ck,* and *ch* stand for the *k* sound in these words.

cat   duck   ache

Write the word in the sentence with /k/. Circle the letter or letters that stand for /k/.

1. Where is my other green sock?   sock
2. My stomach feels full.   stomach
3. The chorus sang a happy song.   chorus
4. This bucket of water is heavy.   bucket
5. My tooth ached all night.   ached
6. Have you ever been camping?   camping
7. Someone left a red jacket on the bus.   jacket
8. How high did he count?   count
9. My friend drives a big truck.   truck
10. What is the name of that chord?   chord
11. The traffic was heavy today.   traffic
12. I heard the echo of my voice.   echo
13. My uncle lives in Ohio.   uncle
14. What caused the lamp to fall?   caused
15. We need an anchor for the boat.   anchor

Notes for Home: Your child identified and wrote words with /k/ spelled *c, ck,* or *ch.*
Home Activity: Have your child choose two /k/ words he or she wrote on the page and use the words in a sentence.

107

Panel 4 (page 108)

Name_____   **Review r-Controlled Vowels ar, er, ir, or, and ur**

The letters *ar, er, ir, or,* and *ur* stand for the vowel sounds in these words.

car   her   bird   horn   turn

Write the word that belongs in each statement. Then write the letters that stand for the vowel-*r* sound.

nurse	star	circus	verses	storm
barn	ferns	horse	birthday	fur

1. Farmer: "Every morning I let the cows out of the _barn_."   ar
2. Doctor: "The _nurse_ will give you your shot."   ur
3. Astronomer: "Light from that _star_ takes millions of light-years to reach Earth."   ar
4. Vet: "You need to brush your cat's _fur_."   ur
5. Gardener: "I find that _ferns_ grow best in shady, moist places."   er
6. Baker: "Do you want vanilla or chocolate icing on this _birthday_ cake?"   ir
7. Ringmaster: "Welcome to the _circus_."   ir
8. Jockey: "I knew my _horse_ could win the race."   or
9. Poet: "My new poem has seven _verses_."   er
10. Weather Forecaster: "We are expecting a major _storm_ with heavy rain and high winds."   or

Notes for Home: Your child wrote words with *r*-controlled vowels. **Home Activity:** Help your child make up a new sentence for each word written on the page.

108

Page 109

Name _____

The letters *air* and *are* stand for the vowel sound in these words.

chair   **dare**

Write the words in the correct order to make sentences. Circle the words with the vowel patterns *air* and *are*.

1. careful Be walking the across street.
   Be (careful) walking across the street.

2. scared That growling dog me.
   That growling dog (scared) me.

3. friends to fair Our the drove us.
   Our friends drove us to the (fair).

4. takes her good She care of goldfish.
   She takes good (care) of her goldfish.

5. ice slick the made The stairs.
   The ice made the (stairs) slick.

6. very has ears A long hare.
   A (hare) has very long ears.

7. baby silky The blond has hair.
   The baby has silky blond (hair).

8. a pair got new shoes I of.
   I got a new (pair) of shoes.

9. have a tire spare in Always the car.
   Always have a (spare) tire in the car.

10. a flair has for Rosa painting.
    Rosa has a (flair) for painting.

Notes for Home: Your child wrote sentences with *air* and *are* words.
Home Activity: Take turns with your child writing a scrambled sentence with an *air* or *are* word and having the other person unscramble the sentence.

109

Page 110

Name _____

The letters *ear* and *our* stand for the vowel sounds in these words.

near   **learn**   **gourd**

Write the word that goes with the clue. Write the letters that stand for the vowel-*r* sound.

early	hear	mourn	course	fourth
four	source	search	year	court
fear	earth	earn	pour	dear

1. do this with your ears	hear	ear
2. the number after three	four	our
3. where something comes from	source	our
4. 52 weeks in this	year	ear
5. the opposite of *late*	early	ear
6. a path followed	course	our
7. to look for	search	ear
8. a word for *soil*	earth	ear
9. do this with milk	pour	our
10. a scared feeling	fear	ear
11. feel sad about something	mourn	our
12. to make money	earn	ear
13. a place with judges	court	our
14. the place after third	fourth	our
15. word to begin a letter	dear	ear

Notes for Home: Your child wrote words with the vowel patterns *ear* and *our*.
Home Activity: Help your child make a list of words with the vowel sounds and patterns in *near, learn,* and *four.* Have your child read the words and name words that rhyme.

110

Page 111

Name _____

When a prefix is added to the beginning of a word, it changes the meaning of the word.

possible	able to be done	**im**possible	not able to be done
honest	truthful	**dis**honest	not truthful
living	alive	**non**living	not alive

Write the word from the box that has the prefix and meaning shown.

imperfect   disloyal   immovable   nonstop   nonbreakable
disappear   nonresident   disapprove   impolite   impatient

1. dis + faithful   disloyal

2. im + able to change its place   immovable

3. non + able to be broken   nonbreakable

4. im + showing manners   impolite

5. dis + come into sight   disappear

6. dis + be in favor of   disapprove

7. non + a person living in a place   nonresident

8. non + will not halt   nonstop

9. im + having no mistakes   imperfect

10. im + willing to wait   impatient

Notes for Home: Your child wrote words with the prefixes *im-*, *dis-*, and *non-*.
Home Activity: Have your child name some other words with the prefixes *im-*, *dis-*, and *non-* and tell what the words mean. Use a dictionary for help.

111

Page 112

Name _____

When a prefix is added to the beginning of a word, the spelling of the word does not change.

im + polite = impolite
dis + appear = disappear
non + living = nonliving

Add *im-*, *dis-*, or *non-* to each word to make a new word. Write the new word.

1. possible   impossible   2. please   displease
3. agree   disagree   4. stop   nonstop
5. fiction   nonfiction   6. practical   impractical
7. honest   dishonest   8. fat   nonfat
9. patient   impatient   10. proper   improper

Sort the words you wrote above according to their prefixes.

dis-   **non-**

11. disagree   14. nonfiction
12. dishonest   15. nonstop
13. displease   16. nonfat

im-

17. impossible
18. impatient
19. impractical
20. improper

Notes for Home: Your child added the prefixes *im-*, *dis-*, and *non-* to words.
Home Activity: Take turns with your child using the words he or she wrote on the page in oral sentences.

112

Prefixes, such as *im-*, *dis-*, and *non-*, change the meanings of words.

im + polite	**im**polite	not polite
dis + honest	**dis**honest	not honest
non + breakable	**non**breakable	not breakable

Write the opposite of each word by circling the correct prefix and writing the new word.

	Prefixes		**Word**	**Word with Prefix**
1.	im	(dis)	non	please	displease
2.	(im)	dis	non	possible	impossible
3.	im	dis	(non)	stop	nonstop
4.	im	(dis)	non	like	dislike
5.	(im)	dis	non	patient	impatient
6.	im	dis	(non)	living	nonliving
7.	im	(dis)	non	loyal	disloyal
8.	(im)	dis	non	practical	impractical
9.	im	dis	(non)	sense	nonsense
10.	im	(dis)	non	approve	disapprove

Notes for Home: Your child added the prefixes *im-*, *dis-*, and *non-* to words.
Home Activity: Help your child name words that are opposites. Use some words that begin with *im-*, *dis-*, and *non-*.

113

Plural nouns can be made in several ways.

• The plurals of most nouns are formed by adding *-s* or *-es*.
• If a noun ends in a vowel and *y*, *s* is added.
• If a noun ends in a consonant and *y*, the *y* is changed to *i*, and *-es* is added.
• The plurals of words ending in *s*, *ss*, *x*, *ch*, or *sh* are formed by adding *-es*.

Write the plural form of the word in parentheses.

1. Our (family) like to have picnics. _____ families
2. We all help make the picnic (lunch). _____ lunches
3. My sister likes fruit (salad). _____ salads
4. I like chicken (sandwich). _____ sandwiches
5. Dad says we must always bring (cherry). _____ cherries
6. Mom loves cool (glass) of lemonade. _____ glasses
7. We usually have the picnics on (holiday). _____ holidays
8. Each family brings (box) of balls and bats. _____ boxes
9. The boys play on (team) against the girls. _____ teams
10. These (day) together are wonderful. _____ days

Notes for Home: Your child formed the plurals of nouns. **Home Activity:** Together talk about food you both like to eat at picnics. Use plurals as you talk.

114

Some nouns have special plurals.

• The plurals of nouns that end in *f* and *fe* are formed by changing *f* or *fe* to *v* and adding *-es*.   shel**f**   shel**ves**
• Sometimes a new word is used for the plural.   man   men
• Sometimes the singular and plural forms are the same.   scissors   scissors

Sort the words to show how each plural was formed.

teeth	women	calves	mice	knives
leaves	sheep	children	wolves	moose
deer	geese	loaves	selves	feet

The *f* or *fe* was changed to *v*. Then *-es* was added.

1.	leaves	2.	calves
3.	loaves	4.	wolves
5.	selves	6.	knives

A new word was used.

7.	teeth	8.	women
9.	geese	10.	children
11.	mice	12.	feet

The same word is used for singular and plural.

| 13. | deer | 14. | sheep |
| | | 15. | moose |

Notes for Home: Your child sorted words to show how plurals were formed.
Home Activity: Work together with your child to add more words to the lists.

115

When adding the ending *-ed* or *-ing* to words, sometimes a spelling change is needed.

no change	jump	jump**ed**	jump**ing**
drop the final *e*	hope	hop**ed**	hop**ing**
double the final consonant	stop	stop**ped**	stop**ping**
change final *y* to *i*	cry	cr**ied**	
no change	cry	cry**ing**	

Add the ending shown. Write the new word.

Make No Spelling Change

1. watch (ed) watched
2. lift (ing) lifting
3. pack (ed) packed
4. try (ing) trying
5. deny (ing) denying

Drop the Final *e*

6. like (ed) liked
7. save (ed) saved
8. smile (ing) smiling
9. tire (ed) tired
10. shine (ing) shining

Double the Final Consonant

11. plan (ed) planned
12. drip (ed) dripped
13. run (ing) running
14. swim (ing) swimming
15. get (ing) getting

Change *y* to *i*

16. dry (ed) dried
17. worry (ed) worried
18. supply (ed) supplied
19. try (ed) tried
20. hurry (ing) hurrying

Notes for Home: Your child added *-ed* and *-ing* to words. **Home Activity:** Together look through a newspaper or book to find words ending in *-ed* or *-ing*. Have your child tell whether a spelling change was needed when the ending was added to each word.

116

Answers **179**

When the endings *-er* and *-est* are added to words, a spelling change may be needed.

1. no change	great	great**er**	great**est**
2. drop the final *e*	large	larg**er**	larg**est**
3. double the final consonant	big	big**ger**	big**gest**
4. change final *y* to *i*	happy	happ**ier**	happ**iest**

Write the opposite of each word. Use words from the list. Write **1, 2, 3,** or **4** to show what spelling change, if any, was needed when the ending was added to the answer word.

bigger	easier	hottest	saddest	largest
lightest	driest	youngest	shortest	widest

1. tallest

____shortest____ 1

3. smaller

____bigger____ 3

5. coldest

____hottest____ 3

7. harder

____easier____ 4

9. narrowest

____widest____ 2

2. happiest

____saddest____ 3

4. darkest

____lightest____ 1

6. smallest

____largest____ 2

8. oldest

____youngest____ 1

10. wettest

____driest____ 4

Notes for Home: Your child wrote words with *-er* and *-est*. **Home Activity:** Name a word ending in *-er* or *-est*, and have your child give its opposite. Then have your child name an *-er* or *-est* word and you give its opposite.

117

The ending *-er* can be added to words to make them mean "more." The ending *-est* can be added to words to make them mean "most."

deep   deep**er** (more deep)   deep**est** (most deep)

Write the *-er* and *-est* forms of each word. Remember to make these spelling changes if they are needed.

drop the final *e*	large	larg**er**	larg**est**
double the final consonant	big	big**ger**	big**gest**
change final *y* to *i*	happy	happ**ier**	happ**iest**

Word	**More**	**Most**
1. slow	slower	slowest
2. funny	funnier	funniest
3. sad	sadder	saddest
4. lazy	lazier	laziest
5. flat	flatter	flattest
6. brave	braver	bravest
7. clean	cleaner	cleanest
8. hot	hotter	hottest
9. easy	easier	easiest
10. tame	tamer	tamest

Notes for Home: Your child wrote words with *-er* and *-est*. **Home Activity:** Work together with your child. Choose a word from the page. Use all three forms in a sentence like this: *I was slow, she was slower, but he was slowest of all.*

118

The letters *c, ck,* and *ch* spell the *k* sound in these words.

can   du**ck**   a**ch**e

Underline the word in each group that has /k/. In the box, write the letter or letters that stand for /k/ in the word you underlined.

1. cover
city | c |
ice

2. chair
echo | ch |
inch

3. lock
cheer | ck |
pencil

4. cent
face | c |
uncle

5. chord
chain | ch |
teach

6. peace
stick | ck |
cheese

7. fact
center | c |
dance

8. chase
anchor | ch |
reach

9. each
lettuce | ck |
pocket

10. decide
fancy | c |
music

Notes for Home: Your child identified words with /k/ spelled *c, ck,* and *ch*. **Home Activity:** Take turns with your child giving a meaning clue or a synonym for each underlined word and having the other person name the word.

119

The letters *c, ck,* and *ch* spell /k/ in *color, dock,* and *ache*.

Write the word that goes with the two words shown. Write the letter or letters that stand for /k/.

cousin	corn	rock	cover	stomach
jacket	complete	truck	cool	bucket
colt	chorus	anchor	duck	trick

1. car, bus

____truck____ ck

3. beans, peas

____corn____ c

5. heart, lungs

____stomach____ ch

7. joke, prank

____trick____ ck

9. aunt, uncle

____cousin____ c

11. cold, chilly

____cool____ c

13. stone, pebble

____rock____ ck

2. mast, deck

____anchor____ ch

4. pail, can

____bucket____ ck

6. coat, sweater

____jacket____ ck

8. lid, top

____cover____ c

10. calf, lamb

____colt____ c

12. singers, choir

____chorus____ ch

14. finish, end

____complete____ c

15. goose, swan

____duck____ ck

Notes for Home: Your child wrote words in which /k/ is spelled *c, ck,* or *ch*. **Home Activity:** Take turns with your child naming three things that go together in some way.

120

Panel 1 (page 121)

Name _____   Digraph *wh*; Consonant /h/: *wh*

The letters *wh* stand for the sounds at the beginning of these words.

       what   **wh**o

Read each word. Circle *what* if the *wh* in the word sounds like the *wh* in *what*.
Circle *who* if the *wh* in the word sounds like the *wh* in *who*.

1. white — (what) who
2. why — (what) who
3. whole — what (who)
4. wheat — (what) who
5. whom — what (who)
6. wheel — (what) who
7. whose — what (who)
8. when — (what) who
9. where — (what) who
10. which — (what) who
11. whoever — what (who)
12. while — (what) who
13. whirl — (what) who
14. wholesome — what (who)
15. whistle — (what) who

Notes for Home: Your child identified words in which *wh* stands for two different sounds.
Home Activity: Together use the words *who*, *what*, *when*, *where*, and *why* to ask each other questions.

121

Panel 2 (page 122)

Name _____   Digraph *wh*; Consonant /h/: *wh*

The letters *wh* stand for the beginning sound in *wheel*.
The letters *wh* stand for the beginning sound in *whole*.

Write the words in which *wh* stands for the sound in *wheel* around the wheel. Write the words in which *wh* stands for the sound in *whole* on the loaf of whole-wheat bread.

white	who	when	why	whoever
what	where	whirl	whose	whom

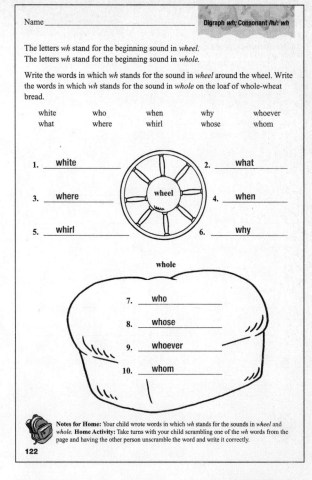

1. white
2. what
3. where
4. when
5. whirl
6. why

whole

7. who
8. whose
9. whoever
10. whom

Notes for Home: Your child wrote words in which *wh* stands for the sounds in *wheel* and *whole*. **Home Activity:** Take turns with your child scrambling one of the *wh* words from the page and having the other person unscramble the word and write it correctly.

122

Panel 3 (page 123)

Name _____   Digraph *wh*; Consonant /h/: *wh*

The letters *wh* stand for the beginning sounds in *what* and *who*.

Write the word from the box that rhymes with the numbered word. Then write *what* if the word you wrote has a *wh* that sounds like the *wh* in *what*. Write *who* if the word has a *wh* that sounds like the *wh* in *who*.

Word box:
whip, whale, whole, when, where, why, whose, whim, whom, wheat

1. ten — when / what
2. try — why / what
3. lose — whose / who
4. lip — whip / what
5. mole — whole / who
6. sale — whale / what
7. loom — whom / who
8. seat — wheat / what
9. pair — where / what
10. skim — whim / what

Notes for Home: Your child wrote words with *wh*. **Home Activity:** Have your child name other rhyming words for the words in the box.

123

Panel 4 (page 124)

Name _____   Review Prefixes *im-*, *dis-*, and *non-*

The prefixes *im-*, *dis-*, and *non-* can be added to the beginnings of words.

    im + polite = impolite
    dis + appear = disappear
    non + living = nonliving

Find and circle a word with the prefix *im-*, *dis-*, or *non-* in each group of letters.

1. a d r (impossible) r s
2. p r e (nonstop) m e n t s
3. b e a b t e t (distrust)
4. (disagree) a g l e r e d
5. s o r (imperfect) e t o n

Write the words you circled above to complete the sentences.

6. The cracked glass is **imperfect**.
7. I **disagree** with what you said.
8. The acrobat did a trick that looked **impossible** to do.
9. She is a person I **distrust**.
10. The plane flies **nonstop** to Dallas.

Notes for Home: Your child identified and wrote words with prefixes. **Home Activity:** Take turns with your child making up a different sentence for each of the circled words.

124

Top-left panel

Name _____

The prefixes *im-*, *dis-*, and *non-* change the meaning but not the spelling of a word.

im + polite = impolite   not polite
dis + honest = dishonest   not honest
non + breakable = nonbreakable   not breakable

Add *im-*, *dis-*, or *non-* to make a new word. Then write the meaning of the new word.   **Answers will vary.**

1. __im__ possible   not possible
2. __dis__ loyal   not loyal
3. __non__ stop   making no stops
4. __im__ patient   not patient
5. __dis__ trust   does not trust
6. __im__ perfect   not perfect
7. __non__ fiction   not fiction
8. __dis__ pleased   not pleased
9. __non__ living   not living
10. __dis__ liked   does not like

Notes for Home: Your child added prefixes to words and wrote meaning clues for the new words. **Home Activity:** Have your child look in newspapers and magazines for words with the prefixes *im-*, *dis-*, and *non-* and help him or her tell what each word means.

125

Top-right panel

Name _____

The vowels *a, e, i, o,* and *u* can stand for the vowel sound heard in unaccented syllables. This vowel sound is called the schwa sound. Listen for the schwa sound in these words.

about   taken   pencil   melon   circus

Write the vowel that stands for the schwa sound in each word.

1. ago __a__   2. kitchen __e__   3. today __o__
4. focus __u__   5. cabin __i__   6. number __e__
7. major __o__   8. allow __a__   9. useful __u__
10. dollar __a__   11. fallen __e__   12. actor __o__

Match the beginning of each sentence to its ending. Write each sentence. Circle two words with the schwa sound.

I got two gallons of milk   as citrus fruit.
Lemons are known   tuna salad sandwich.
I made one tasty   at Al's grocery store.

13. I got two (gallons) of milk at Al's (grocery) store.
14. (Lemons) are known as (citrus) fruit.
15. I made one tasty (tuna) (salad) sandwich.

Notes for Home: Your child identified words with the schwa sound. **Home Activity:** Have your child tell you how he or she thinks a favorite dish is prepared. Listen for and call attention to words used that have the schwa sound.

126

Bottom-left panel

Name _____

The vowels *a, e, i, o,* and *u* can stand for the schwa sound. Listen for the schwa sound in these words.

about   taken   pencil   lemon   circus

Write the words in each box that have the schwa sound.

Animals
zebra   1. zebra
horse   2. otter
otter   3. parakeet
parakeet

Clothes
shirt   4. trousers
trousers   5. sweater
sweater   6. slippers
slippers

Number Words
seven   7. seven
thirty   8. eleven
eleven   9. hundred
hundred

Buildings
skyscraper   10. skyscraper
cabin   11. cabin
apartment   12. apartment
house

Food
apple   13. apple
banana   14. banana
bread   15. chicken
chicken

Notes for Home: Your child identified words with the schwa sound. **Home Activity:** With your child, name other words that could be included in each category. Check to see if any of them have the schwa sound.

127

Bottom-right panel

Name _____

The letters *a, e, i, o,* and *u* stand for the schwa sound in these words.

about   taken   robin   lemon   circus

Write the word for each picture. Then write the letter that stands for the schwa sound.

sweater   apple   pencil   carrot   cactus
cabin   seven   zebra   walrus   wagon

1.  zebra   a
2.  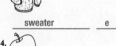 sweater   e
3.  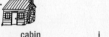 wagon   o
4. 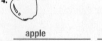 apple   e
5. cabin   i
6.  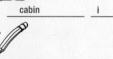 cactus   u
7.  pencil   i
8.  seven   e
9. carrot   o
10.  walrus   u

Notes for Home: Your child wrote words and the letters that stand for the schwa sound. **Home Activity:** With your child, look in a magazine for pictures of things whose names have the schwa sound.

128

Name_____

The letters *wh* stand for the beginning sounds in these words.

what   **who**

Put a check by each word in which *wh* stands for the same sound as in the word at the top of the box.

what		who	
1. white	✔	11. whom	✔
2. whale	✔	12. while	___
3. wheel	✔	13. wharf	___
4. when	✔	14. whoever	✔
5. whole	___	15. which	___
6. where	✔	16. wholesome	✔
7. whether	✔	17. why	___
8. whose	___	18. wholly	✔
9. whistle	✔	19. whip	___
10. whirl	✔	20. wholesale	✔

Write a word you checked above to complete each sentence.

21. The kitten is black with _____white_____ paws.

22. Wheat bread is often thought to be a _____wholesome_____ food.

23. To _____whom_____ is this gift to be sent?

24. The referee blew a _____whistle_____ because of a foul.

25. A _____whale_____ is a large sea mammal.

Notes for Home: Your child identified words in *wh* stands for two different sounds. **Home Activity:** Help your child choose five words from the boxes and put them in alphabetical order.

129

Name_____

The letters *wh* stand for two different sounds: the sound heard in *what* and the sound heard in *who*.

Circle the *wh* word or words in each question. Then answer the question. If you are not sure, make up your own answer.

1. (Where) did Little Miss Muffet sit?   Answers will vary.
   She sat on a tuffet._____

2. (Who) did Simple Simon meet?
   He met a pieman.

3. (Whose) mittens were lost?
   The three little kittens' mittens were lost.

4. (What) followed Mary to school?
   Mary's lamb followed her to school,

5. (Why) did Jack and Jill go up a hill?
   They went to fetch a pail of water.

6. (Where) was the cow (while) Little Boy Blue was asleep?
   It was in the corn.

7. By (when) was the cobbler to have the shoe mended?
   He was to have it mended by half-past two.

8. For (whom) did Old Mother Hubbard go to the cupboard?
   She went to the cupboard for her dog.

9. (Which) animal—the cow or the cat—jumped over the moon?
   The cow jumped over the moon.

10. (Who) wanted to see (whether) they could put Humpty Dumpty together again?
    All the king's horses and men did.

Notes for Home: Your child wrote words with *wh*. **Home Activity:** Say some nursery rhymes with your child such as "Mary Had a Little Lamb" or "Little Miss Muffet." Point out any *wh* words you say.

130

Name_____

To count the number of syllables in a word, count the number of vowel sounds you hear.

side	one vowel sound	=	one syllable
teacher	two vowel sounds	=	two syllables
uniform	three vowel sounds	=	three syllables

Look at and say the picture name. Write the number of vowels you **see** in the first box. Write the number of vowels you **hear** in the second box. Write the number of syllables in the word in the third box.

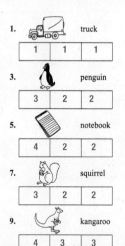

1. truck
| 1 | 1 | 1 |

2. chicken
| 2 | 2 | 2 |

3. penguin
| 3 | 2 | 2 |

4. peach
| 2 | 1 | 1 |

5. notebook
| 4 | 2 | 2 |

6. elephant
| 3 | 3 | 3 |

7. squirrel
| 3 | 2 | 2 |

8. butterfly
| 3 | 3 | 3 |

9. kangaroo
| 4 | 3 | 3 |

10. dinosaur
| 4 | 3 | 3 |

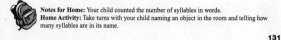
Notes for Home: Your child counted the number of syllables in words. **Home Activity:** Take turns with your child naming an object in the room and telling how many syllables are in its name.

131

Name_____

Sometimes dividing a word into parts can help you read a word you do not know.

• Divide between the two smaller words in a compound word.
  doghouse   dog/house

• Divide between a prefix, a suffix, or an ending and the base word.
  re/read   pay/ment   un/fold/ed   care/less/ness

Rewrite the words. Use slashes to show where to divide the words.

1. graceful	grace/ful	2. birthday	birth/day
3. popcorn	pop/corn	4. softly	soft/ly
5. unlucky	un/luck/y	6. inside	in/side
7. breakfast	break/fast	8. weekend	week/end
9. maybe	may/be	10. unpack	un/pack
11. bedroom	bed/room	12. unsafe	un/safe
13. airport	air/port	14. cheerful	cheer/ful
15. distrustful	dis/trust/ful	16. unkindness	un/kind/ness
17. unsafely	un/safe/ly	18. backyard	back/yard
19. playfully	play/ful/ly	20. moonlight	moon/light

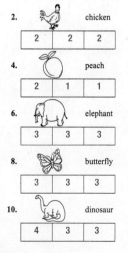
Notes for Home: Your child divided compound words and words with affixes into syllables. **Home Activity:** Help your child list some compound words and divide each word into syllables by drawing slashes between syllables.

132

Name_____

Sometimes looking for small parts in a big word can help you read the word.

- Look for affixes. **un**/like/**ly**   **re**/place/**ment**
- Look for little words you already know. **out**/ward   **ten**/sion
- Look for familiar vowel patterns. mon/**soon**   pro/**ceed**   re/**bate**

Write the syllables of each word on the lines below. One syllable is already written for you.

independent	emergency	embarrassment
receptionist	spitefulness	reconstruction
neighborhood	convenience	establishment
photosynthesis	electromagnet	gymnastics
splendidly	prescription	unhappiness

1. __splen__ / __did__ / ly
2. es / __tab__ / __lish__ / __ment__
3. __pho__ / __to__ / __syn__ / the / __sis__
4. __gym__ / __nas__ / tics
5. __un__ / __hap__ / pi / __ness__
6. __re__ / __cep__ / __tion__ / ist
7. __e__ / __lec__ / tro / __mag__ / __net__
8. em / __bar__ / __rass__ / __ment__
9. __re__ / __con__ / struc / __tion__
10. __spite__ / ful / __ness__
11. __con__ / __ven__ / i / __ence__
12. __in__ / de / __pen__ / __dent__
13. __pre__ / scrip / __tion__
14. __e__ / __mer__ / __gen__ / cy
15. __neigh__ / bor / __hood__

Notes for Home: Your child divided words into syllables. **Home Activity:** Have your child look through a newspaper article and highlight words with three or more syllables.

133

Name_____

When adding the ending -ed or -ing, the spelling of a word sometimes has to be changed.

start, started, starting	no change
hope, hoped, hoping	drop the final e
stop, stopped, stopping	double the final consonant
try, tried	change y to i
try, trying	no change

Add -ed or -ing to each word in the box to make a word that completes each sentence. Write the new word.

swim	fly	hurry	chase	laugh
hop	paint	move	cry	study

1. She __studied__ hard for the spelling test.
2. Let's go __swimming__ in the pool to cool off.
3. Who __moved__ into the house next to yours?
4. The unhappy baby started __crying__ again.
5. In the movie, a kangaroo was __hopping__ over a fence.
6. Our dog __chased__ the squirrel up the tree.
7. I like __painting__ pictures of dinosaurs with my watercolor set.
8. We saw some geese __flying__ south.
9. I __hurried__ outside, so I would not miss the bus.
10. We were all __laughing__ at the silly joke.

Notes for Home: Your child added the endings -ed and -ing to words, making spelling changes where needed. **Home Activity:** Take turns with your child telling about something you like to do. See how many -ed and -ing words you use.

134

Name_____

Adding -er to some words can make them mean "more."
Add -est to some words can make them mean "most."

sad   sadd**er** (more sad)   sadd**est** (most sad)

Add -er or -est to make each word mean "more" or "most." Remember to make spelling changes if necessary.

1. most big
   biggest
2. more wide
   wider
3. most dry
   driest
4. more light
   lighter
5. most tall
   tallest
6. most large
   largest
7. more heavy
   heavier
8. more old
   older
9. more tame
   tamer
10. more quick
   quicker
11. most flat
   flattest
12. most wet
   wettest
13. more brave
   braver
14. most easy
   easiest
15. more muddy
   muddier

Notes for Home: Your child wrote words ending in -er and -est. **Home Activity:** Have your child list ten words that end with -er and ten words that end with -est and then use "more" and "most" to tell what each word means.

135

Name_____

The letters aw, au, and al stand for the vowel sound in these words.

draw   cause   hall

Write the letters that stand for the vowel sound you hear in *draw* in each word. Underline *beginning, middle,* or *end* to show where you hear that vowel sound.

1. raw __aw__
   beginning   middle   (end)
2. talk __al__
   beginning   (middle)   end
3. small __al__
   beginning   (middle)   end
4. awesome __aw__
   (beginning)   middle   end
5. lawn __aw__
   beginning   (middle)   end
6. thaw __aw__
   beginning   middle   (end)
7. paw __aw__
   beginning   middle   (end)
8. salt __al__
   beginning   (middle)   end
9. stall __al__
   beginning   (middle)   end
10. falling __al__
   beginning   (middle)   end
11. sauce __au__
   beginning   (middle)   end
12. pause __au__
   beginning   (middle)   end
13. claws __aw__
   beginning   (middle)   end
14. walk __al__
   beginning   (middle)   end
15. because __au__
   beginning   (middle)   end

Notes for Home: In this activity, your child identified the aw, au, and al vowel patterns in words. **Home Activity:** Take turns with your child naming a word on the page and then naming another word on the page with the same vowel sound and spelling.

136

---

184   Answers

The same vowel sound can be spelled by different letter pairs.

draw   cause   hall

Add the letters *aw*, *au*, or *al* to make the words in the list.

baseball	draw	author	auto	false
hawk	fall	chalk	straw	faucet

1. h _a_ _w_ k   2. dr _a_ _w_

3. f _a_ _l_ l   4. _a_ _u_ to

5. ch _a_ _l_ k   6. str _a_ _w_

7. baseb _a_ _l_ l   8. _a_ _u_ thor

9. f _a_ _l_ se   10. f _a_ _u_ cet

Write the word from above that goes with each clue.

11. Use this to write on the board. _____ chalk _____

12. A pitcher throws this. _____ baseball _____

13. This is a kind of bird. _____ hawk _____

14. This is another word for *car.* _____ auto _____

15. Turn on water with this. _____ faucet _____

16. To make a picture, do this. _____ draw _____

17. It is the opposite of *true.* _____ false _____

18. You can drink through this. _____ straw _____

19. If you trip, you might do this. _____ fall _____

20. This person writes books. _____ author _____

Notes for Home: Your child identified and wrote words with the *aw*, *au*, and *al* vowel patterns. **Home Activity:** Both you and your child should draw a picture for one of the words on the page. Together tell a story to go with each picture.

Draw, cause, and *hall* all have the same vowel sound. But different letters stand for the vowel sound in each word.

Write the word that belongs in each group. Then write the letters that stand for the vowel sound you hear in *draw.*

auto	pause	August	chalk	autumn
baseball	walnut	small	draw	also
hawk	author	straw	auditorium	gnaw

1. little, tiny, _small_   _al_

2. bus, truck, _auto_   _au_

3. paint, color, _draw_   _aw_

4. football, basketball, _baseball_   _al_

5. wait, rest, _pause_   _au_

6. board, eraser, _chalk_   _al_

7. arena, theater, _auditorium_   _au_

8. eagle, falcon, _hawk_   _aw_

9. bite, chew, _gnaw_   _aw_

10. acorn, cashew, _walnut_   _al_

11. spring, summer, _autumn_   _au_

12. in addition, too, _also_   _al_

13. writer, poet, _author_   _au_

14. June, July, _August_   _au_

15. grass, hay, _straw_   _aw_

Notes for Home: Your child wrote words with the *aw*, *au*, and *al* vowel patterns. **Home Activity:** Help your child make up other groups of three words and tell how the words go together.

The vowels—*a, e, i, o, u*—can stand for a vowel sound called the schwa sound. You hear the schwa sound in unaccented syllables. Listen for the schwa sound in these words.

zebra   sweater   pencil   lemon   circus

Write each word under the word that has the same spelling for the schwa sound.

grocery	tuna	eleven	carrot	citrus
awful	tractor	cabin	salad	focus
cabinet	vessel	stencil	allow	actor

zebra   sweater

1. _tuna_   4. _grocery_
2. _salad_   5. _vessel_
3. _allow_   6. _eleven_

pencil   lemon

7. _cabinet_   10. _tractor_
8. _cabin_   11. _carrot_
9. _stencil_   12. _actor_

circus

13. _awful_
14. _citrus_
15. _focus_

Notes for Home: Your child sorted words according to the spelling of their schwa sound. **Home Activity:** Help your child use a dictionary to find ten more words with the schwa sound. (The schwa symbol is /ə/ in a dictionary.)

The vowels *a, e, i, o,* and *u* stand for the schwa sound in these words.

about   taken   pencil   lemon   circus

Complete each rhyme by writing a word from the list with the schwa sound. Circle the letter that stands for the schwa sound.

tractor	liver	ago	wagon	awful
cabinet	eleven	bacon	liner	slippers

1. Lots of white, fluffy snow
   Fell not too long _ago_.   (a) e i o u

2. There are tiny silver zippers
   On the fancy bedroom _slippers_.   a (e) i o u

3. I ate only a tiny sliver
   Of the big piece of _liver_.   a (e) i o u

4. Dad used the Internet
   To buy a wooden _cabinet_.   a e (i) o u

5. In the movie the actor
   Had to drive a big green _tractor_.   a e i (o) u

6. She just turned seven,
   But I am not _eleven_.   a (e) i o u

7. There is nothing finer
   Than a trip on an ocean _liner_.   a (e) i o u

8. The gentle striped dragon
   Was pulling a _wagon_.   a e i (o) u

9. So much gum all in one jawful
   Gave me a pain that was _awful_.   a e i o (u)

10. If I am not mistaken,
    That wonderful smell is _bacon_.   a e i (o) u

Notes for Home: Your child wrote words with the schwa sound to complete rhymes. **Home Activity:** Take turns with your child choosing another word with the schwa sound and making up a rhyme for the word.

Answers **185**

Name_____

The letters *ui* and *ew* stand for the vowel sound in these words

bruise   **blew**

Write the word from the box that means the same as the clue. Then circle the letters *ui* or *ew* that stand for the vowel sound.

newspaper	suit	crew	new	drew
juice	grew	cruise	fruit	chew

1. sail from place to place — cruise

2. what someone did who is now taller — grew

3. apples, bananas, and grapes, for example — fruit

4. never used — new

5. liquid from an orange or other fruit — juice

6. jacket and pants that go together — suit

7. something to read that has today's information — newspaper

8. people who work together as a team — crew

9. what someone did who sketched a picture — drew

10. what the dog did to a bone — chew

Notes for Home: Your child wrote words with the vowel patterns *ui* and *ew*.
Home Activity: Have your child choose some words from the box and use them to begin a story. Then take turns adding to the story.

141

Name_____

In *suit*, the vowel sound is spelled *ui*. In *new*, the same vowel sound is spelled *ew*.

Follow the directions to make new words. Then circle the letters that stand for the vowel sound.

1. Start with **bruise.**
   Take away the **b.**
   Add **c.** Write the new word.
   cruise

2. Start with **crew.**
   Take away the **cr.**
   Add **dr.** Write the new word.
   drew

3. Start with **fruit.**
   Take away the **fr.**
   Add **s.** Write the new word.
   suit

4. Start with **blew.**
   Take away the **bl.**
   Add **ch.** Write the new word.
   chew

5. Start with **flew.**
   Take away the **fl.**
   Add **gr.** Write the new word.
   grew

6. Start with **judo.**
   Take away the **do.**
   Add **ice.** Write the new word.
   juice

7. Start with **grew.**
   Take away the **gr.**
   Add **bl.** Write the new word.
   blew

8. Start with **drew.**
   Take away the **d.**
   Add **c.** Write the new word.
   crew

9. Start with **suit.**
   Take away the **s.**
   Add **fr.** Write the new word.
   fruit

10. Start with **cruise.**
    Take away the **cr.**
    Add **br.** Write the new word.
    bruise

Notes for Home: Your child wrote words with the vowel patterns *ui* and *ew*.
Home Activity: Have your child use two of the *ui* or *ew* words from the page to write a rhyme.

142

Name_____

The letters *ui* and *ew* stand for the vowel sound in *bruise* and *chew*.

Write the word from the box that completes each phrase. Circle the letters that stand for a vowel sound.

juice	drew	suit	grew	flew
new	fruit	crew	cruise	blew

1. rode my brand- new _____ bike   ui   (ew)

2. _ drew _____ a picture of our cat   ui   (ew)

3. drank some fresh orange juice _____   (ui)   ew

4. ate a banana from a bowl of fruit _____   (ui)   ew

5. the _ crew _____ of the space shuttle   ui   (ew)

6. geese that _ flew _____ over our house   ui   (ew)

7. jacket for a business _ suit _____   (ui)   ew

8. winds that _ blew _____ 40 miles per hour   ui   (ew)

9. _ grew _____ vegetables to eat   ui   (ew)

10. take a _ cruise _____ to Bermuda   (ui)   ew

Notes for Home: Your child wrote words with the *ui* and *ew* vowel patterns.
Home Activity: Take turns with your child making up new phrases or sentences for each word in the box.

143

Name_____

Dividing words into syllables may help you read words you do not know.

- To count the number of syllables in a word, count the number of vowel sounds.
- Divide between the two smaller words in a compound word.
  doghouse   dog/house
- Divide between a prefix, a suffix, or an ending and the base word.
  re/read   go/ing   dis/place/ment   care/less/ness

Write each word under the heading that tells how many syllables it has. Then draw lines to show how to divide each word into syllables.

repayment	distrustful	unkindness	outside	unsafely
crying	unfairness	homework	leadership	playground
sunglasses	displeased	careless	replace	rebuilding
doing	crewmate	mistreatment	playfully	meanwhile

Two-Syllable Words

1. cry/ing   2. do/ing
3. dis/pleased   4. crew/mate
5. home/work   6. care/less
7. out/side   8. re/place
9. play/ground   10. mean/while

Three-Syllable Words

11. re/pay/ment   12. sun/glass/es
13. dis/trust/ful   14. un/fair/ness
15. un/kind/ness   16. mis/treat/ment
17. lead/er/ship   18. play/ful/ly
19. un/safe/ly   20. re/build/ing

Notes for Home: Your child sorted two- and three-syllable words and divided the words into syllables. **Home Activity:** Have your child find some two- and three-syllable words in a newspaper or magazine.

144

---

186 Answers

Panel 1 (page 145)

Sometimes looking for small parts in a big word can help you read the word.

- Look for affixes.   **un**/like/**ly**   re/place/**ment**
- Look for little words you already know.   **out**/ward   ten/sion
- Look for familiar vowel patterns.   mon/**soon**   pro/**ceed**   re/bate

Match each word with a clue. Write the word in syllables.

unhealthy	subtraction	Tennessee	illustrate	imprison
skeleton	televise	reminder	basketball	endlessly
chimpanzee	yesterday	promotion	Washington	pantomime

1. a southern state — Ten / nes / see
2. never stopping — end / less / ly
3. 25 − 11 = 13 — sub / trac / tion
4. gestures without words — pan / to / mime
5. broadcast on TV — tel / e / vise
6. movement to a higher level — pro / mo / tion
7. small ape — chim / pan / zee
8. game played with a large, round ball — bas / ket / ball
9. all the bones in the body — skel / e / ton
10. not well — un / health / y
11. make pictures for — il / lus / trate
12. the day before today — yes / ter / day
13. put in prison — im / pris / on
14. something to help you remember — re / mind / er
15. first U.S. president — Wash / ing / ton

 Notes for Home: Your child divided words into syllables. **Home Activity:** Take turns with your child finding a long word in a story and dividing it into syllables. Be sure to check your answers in a dictionary.

145

Panel 2 (page 146)

When an affix is added to a word, a spelling change may or may not be needed.

- **Prefixes**
  no spelling change   happy   **un**happy
- **Suffixes and Endings**
  no spelling change   go   go**ing**
  drop the final *e*   hope   hop**ing**
  double the final consonant   big   big**ger**
  change *y* to *i*   happy   happ**iness**

Add the affix or affixes shown. Write the new word.

1. The dinner tasted (wonder + ful). — wonderful
2. I could hardly wait to (un + wrap) the gift. — unwrap
3. She sang (happy + ly) all morning. — happily
4. The kitchen faucet is (drip + ing). — dripping
5. The (smile + ing) baby laughed. — smiling
6. I (like + ed) the movie. — liked
7. Where is the (swim + ing) pool? — swimming
8. The sun was shining (bright + ly). — brightly
9. They were (dis + please + ed) with the work. — displeased
10. She slept (un + easy + ly) through the storm. — uneasily

 Notes for Home: Your child added affixes—prefixes, suffixes, and endings—to words. **Home Activity:** Together with your child choose one of the sentences and use it to begin a story. Try to use words with affixes as you tell the story.

146

Panel 3 (page 147)

A word may have one or more affixes added to it.

Prefix	Suffix	Ending	More Than One Affix
disappear	appear**ance**	appear**ing**	**dis**appear**ance**

Write each word to show what affixes were added.

sickness	unhappy	incorrectly	unpacking	repainted
drawing	shortest	distrusted	impolitely	sadly

	Prefix	Base Word	Suffix or Ending
1.		sick	ness
2.		draw	ing
3.	un	happy	
4.		short	est
5.	in	correct	ly
6.	dis	trust	ed
7.	un	pack	ing
8.	im	polite	ly
9.	re	paint	ed
10.		sad	ly

 Notes for Home: Your child identified affixes—prefixes, suffixes, and endings—in words. **Home Activity:** Together with your child look through a favorite book for words with affixes. Take turns naming the base word and the affixes added.

147

Panel 4 (page 148)

When affixes are added to words, a spelling change may be needed.

Underline the word in the sentence that has an affix or affixes added. Then write the base word and the affixes.

1. I disagree with your idea.
   Base Word agree   Affix or Affixes dis
2. That is the biggest snake I have ever seen.
   Base Word big   Affix or Affixes est
3. They cried when they heard the sad story.
   Base Word cry   Affix or Affixes ed
4. I like a movie that is humorous.
   Base Word humor   Affix or Affixes ous
5. She is hoping to go to the park.
   Base Word hope   Affix or Affixes ing
6. Our team was victorious.
   Base Word victory   Affix or Affixes ous
7. Who uncovered the treasure chest?
   Base Word cover   Affix or Affixes un ed
8. Why are you displeased with the book?
   Base Word please   Affix or Affixes dis ed
9. The huge rock is immovable.
   Base Word move   Affix or Affixes im able
10. We sat impatiently because the play did not begin on time.
    Base Word patient   Affix or Affixes im ly

 Notes for Home: Your child identified base words and affixes—prefixes, suffixes, and endings. **Home Activity:** Together with your child look through junk mail for examples of words with affixes. Tell what the base word is and what affixes were added.

148

The letters *aw*, *au*, and *al* stand for the vowel sound in these words.

draw   cause   hall

Draw lines to match two rhyming words with the same spelling for the vowel sound.

1. call — talk
2. walk — law
3. lawn — wall
4. cause — drawn
5. paw — pause

6. claw — dawn
7. salt — halt
8. haul — waltz
9. false — flaw
10. yawn — Paul

Write each pair of words you matched above. Write the letters that stand for the vowel sound.

Words			Vowel Sound
11. call	and	wall	al
12. walk	and	talk	al
13. lawn	and	drawn	aw
14. cause	and	pause	au
15. paw	and	law	aw
16. claw	and	flaw	aw
17. salt	and	halt	al
18. haul	and	Paul	au
19. false	and	waltz	al
20. yawn	and	dawn	aw

Notes for Home: Your child matched rhyming words with *aw*, *au*, and *al*.
Home Activity: Together with your child use pairs of words from the page to make up silly rhymes.

149

The letters *aw*, *au*, and *al* stand for the vowel sound in *draw, cause,* and *hall.*

Write the word that answers the question. Circle the letters that stand for the vowel sound you hear in *draw.*

1. Can chalk or yawns squeak? _____ chalk
2. Does a snake crawl or walk? _____ crawl
3. Could a person drive a straw or an auto? _____ auto
4. Does the lawn or the hall get mowed? _____ lawn
5. Would you call or draw a picture? _____ draw
6. Can an author or an altar write a book? _____ author
7. Is a skyscraper tall or small? _____ tall
8. Would you eat a scrawl or a walnut? _____ walnut
9. Is a horse kept in a crawl or a stall? _____ stall
10. Would you cook sauce or chalk? _____ sauce
11. Do claws or hawks fly? _____ hawks
12. Would you hit a flaw or a baseball? _____ baseball
13. Do you wash laundry or lawyers? _____ laundry
14. Would you turn on a faucet or a pause? _____ faucet
15. Would you sit in an auditorium or a drawer? _____ auditorium

Notes for Home: Your child wrote words with the vowel patterns *aw*, *au*, and *al*.
Home Activity: Take turns with your child choosing a word that was not an answer on the page and asking a question about the word.

150

188 Answers